THE
INSTANT POT
TODDLER FOOD
COOKBOOK

Inspiring | Educating | Creating | Entertaining

Brimming with creative inspiration, how-to projects, and useful information to enrich your everyday life, Quarto Knows is a favorite destination for those pursuing their interests and passions. Visit our site and dig deeper with our books into your area of interest: Quarto Creates, Quarto Cooks, Quarto Homes, Quarto Lives, Quarto Drives, Quarto Explores, Quarto Gifts, or Quarto Kids.

First Published in 2019 by The Harvard Common Press, an imprint of The Quarto Group,
100 Cummings Center, Suite 265-D, Beverly, MA 01915, USA.
T (978) 282-9590 F (978) 283-2742 QuartoKnows.com

The Harvard Common Press titles are also available at discount for retail, wholesale, promotional, and bulk purchase. For details, contact the Special Sales Manager by email at specialsales@quarto.com or by mail at The Quarto Group, Attn: Special Sales Manager, 100 Cummings Center, Suite 265-D, Beverly, MA 01915, USA.

ISBN: 978-1-55832-967-6

Digital edition published in 2019
eISBN: 978-1-55832-968-3

Library of Congress Cataloging-in-Publication Data
Names: Schieving, Barbara, author. | McDaniel, Jennifer, author.
Title: The instant pot toddler food cookbook : wholesome recipes that cook up
   fast-in any brand of electric pressure cooker / Barbara Schieving,
   Jennifer Schieving McDaniel.
Description: Beverly, MA, USA : Harvard Common Press, [2019] | Includes index.
Identifiers: LCCN 2018051330 | ISBN 9781558329676 (trade pbk.)
Subjects: LCSH: Toddlers--Nutrition. | Pressure cooking. | Breastfeeding. |
   Electric cooking. | Baby foods. | LCGFT: Cookbooks.
Classification: LCC RJ216 .S396 2019 | DDC 641.5/6222--dc23 LC record available at https://lccn.loc.gov/2018051330

Cover Image: Shutterstock
Page Layout:Gabi Rosoff
Illustration: Shutterstock

The information in this book is for educational purposes only. It is not intended to replace the advice of a physician or medical practitioner. Please see your health-care provider before beginning any new health program.

THE
INSTANT POT
TODDLER FOOD
COOKBOOK

Wholesome Recipes That Cook Up Fast—in
Any Brand of Electric Pressure Cooker

Barbara Schieving
Jennifer Schieving McDaniel

HARVARD
COMMON
PRESS

CONTENTS

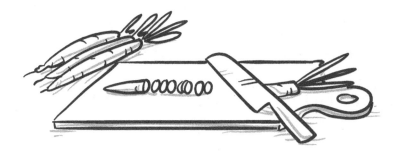

DEDICATION

To all the time-crunched moms and dads doing their best to feed their families nutritious and delicious food, and to our families, friends, and readers who share our passion for pressure cooking and our love of good food—this cookbook is dedicated to you. Thanks for your support.

AUTHORS' NOTE

Whenever possible, we try to cook meals from scratch. Not only is the food better tasting, but we know exactly what ingredients we're eating and can control the levels of salt, sugar, and fat in our foods. When feeding toddlers, it's especially important to ensure they're eating foods that will give them the nutrition they need.

However, toddlers also require a lot of time and energy, so it's not always easy to schedule time to cook from scratch. One of the great things about cooking food in the pressure cooker is that it frees up your time. Because you're not tied to the stove, you can play with your toddler or clean up the toys while dinner cooks.

In this cookbook, we've used the pressure cooker to make it easier and faster to feed your toddler healthy, nutritious meals. We've compiled a mix of kid classics and easily modified adult favorites that will prepare toddlers for eating a wide variety of foods, flavors—and textures. These are recipes your toddler will be excited to eat, colorful foods served in ways that make mealtime fun.

Because our recipes serve three to four people, you're not making a separate meal just for your toddler. Your toddler will truly be eating with the family. That way, they'll gradually learn to love to eat the foods that you love to eat, and family mealtime will be a time that everyone can look forward to.

Thanks for being a part of our pressure cooking journey. We hope you and your toddler enjoy eating these meals together.

—*Barbara Schieving*

—*Jennifer Schieving McDaniel*

INTRODUCTION

The toddler years are a magical time as your babies learn to express themselves, become more playful, and grow into their unique personalities. However, the same things that make these years wonderful can also make them difficult, as these little people begin to assert strong opinions over what they'll wear, do, and eat.

And the thing about eating is that it can seem like toddlers do it *all day long.* The American Academy of Pediatrics recommends toddlers eat three meals a day along with two to three healthy snacks. Some days, it can feel like your toddler is hungry again before you've even cleaned up the previous meal—and that doesn't even account for making healthy meals for yourself!

So, how to cook healthy meals your toddler will eat without losing your mind or spending the entire day in the kitchen? The key is finding quick, easy-to-cook, and healthy meals your toddler will want to eat; in other words, the kind of meals your pressure cooker is naturally suited for.

You'll love the recipes in this book, which are made pressure cooker fast and teach you how to cook main and side dishes at the same time, ultimately getting you out of the kitchen a little quicker.

Our Approach

Your child's food habits start early and are a unique combination of their innate preferences and their personal experiences with food. Just as you teach your toddler to drink from a cup and eat with utensils, you need to teach them to love the healthy foods your family eats. The recipes in this book are designed to do exactly that!

Cook family meals. We don't believe parents need to cook separate meals for toddlers and adults—it's enough work to get one meal on the table! Yet, it can be particularly disheartening to make a big batch of food, only to have your toddler turn up their nose—or worse, throw it on the floor! Therefore, the recipes in this book are designed to make a single meal for a smaller families of three or four, since larger families will likely have grown beyond making meals specifically for their toddlers' tastes.

Customize for toddlers. We've taken our family's favorite recipes and toned down the seasonings and sugar content to introduce your toddler to grown-up food without overwhelming their sensitive palates. (Think of these recipes as training wheels for family eating.) We have also included several points where you can remove a portion specifically for your toddler before finishing the recipe, allowing you to enjoy a grown-up meal and still serve certain foods on the side to help your toddler grow accustomed to the meal.

Make it your way. If you know your toddler hates a certain ingredient, switch it out! Just be sure that when you make a substitution, you're trading for another ingredient that's similar in size, texture, and cooking needs. (For instance, subbing frozen corn for frozen peas would work great, while subbing peas for fresh asparagus or large broccoli florets wouldn't work well.)

The same principles apply for thickeners (use twice as much flour as cornstarch), grains (white rice cooks much faster than brown rice), and meats (ground chicken and ground beef have similar cooking needs, while diced chicken cooks much faster than diced beef or whole chicken breasts). Similarly, if you prefer a sauce or soup thicker or thinner than the one specified, add or reduce the liquids added after pressure cooking.

Spice it up. Many of these recipes give you a range of sugar and spices you can add, allowing you to choose how much of these ingredients you want. These recipes try to strike a good balance between being intentionally mild for your toddlers but not so bland that the parents won't enjoy eating with their toddler. If a dish is too mild for your tastes, add a little extra seasoning to your portion. Or, on the other hand, if the spices are still too much for your toddler, walk things back even further.

Keep it simple. Mealtimes not only test toddlers' adaptability to new textures and flavors, but they also test toddlers' fine motor skills. We've tried to keep these recipes easy for toddlers to eat, including extra-thick breakfasts, soups, and sauces that stick to the spoon or bread when dipped—as necessary, customize the consistency to your family's tastes. In addition, many lunches and dinners go into the pressure cooker bite-sized, minimizing the amount of dicing you have to do once the food is cooked.

A Note about Allergies

For many years, pediatricians recommended delaying introduction of potential allergens like peanuts, eggs, and dairy. However, recent research indicates that early introduction of these foods may actually *lessen* your child's risk of allergies. Since the science isn't settled in this area, we recommend following your pediatrician's advice regarding food introduction.

Out of caution, we've left peanuts out of the cookbook and tree nuts are optional or easily replaced; however, many of our recipes call for eggs and dairy. Omit or substitute any ingredients in this cookbook that your pediatrician has recommended avoiding due to your child's previous reactions to foods or family history of allergens.

Toddler Feeding Basics

Toddler Mealtime Tips

Keep in mind that we're just a mother-daughter team who have done our best to get healthy foods in our toddlers without stressing too much! You'll absolutely want to defer to your pediatrician for specific advice regarding your toddler. However, after all these years feeding kids, we do have a few tricks up our sleeves, supported by recent guidelines from pediatricians and parenting experts.

Keep foods small to avoid choking hazards. As inconvenient as it may be to break out the knife and chop food to bits *every single meal*, it's the safest way to feed your toddler. Quarter carrots, hot dogs, grapes, and tomatoes vertically, then cut into small bites. Chop or mash other fruits, vegetables, breads, and meats into ½-inch (1.3 cm) pieces or smaller. Foods that may be stringy, like beef, orange segments, or celery, should be sliced into very narrow sections and fully separated before serving. Nut butters, including peanut butter, should be thinned with a liquid if served as a dip or spread very thinly on bread.

Toddlers who tend to stuff their mouths with food should only be given a few bites on their plate at a time. And be aware that this isn't a short-term rule—toddlers can't reliably chew their food until age four. We've found a good pair of kitchen shears makes life much easier when it comes to quickly dicing toddler meals.

Offer the same food multiple times and cooked different ways.
Research from the American Academy of Pediatrics has shown that it can take as many as twenty exposures to a new food before a toddler begins to accept it. Preparing food different ways helps you figure out the flavors, colors, and cooking methods your child prefers. For instance, some kids don't like raw veggies, some don't like steamed veggies, some don't like green veggies, and some don't care how the veggie is prepared as long as they can dip it. Keep serving it until you find a way they like it.

Incorporate the five senses. For toddlers, meals are about much more than taste—before they even put the food in their mouths, it has to pass a visual inspection as well as the sniff test. Don't worry, though! Your toddler doesn't expect photo-worthy meals and can be happy with dividing the meals into separate compartments. (This principle led directly to our approach in the lunch section of the cookbook where each of the major ingredients of a grown-up meal is served à la carte in separated trays.)

Keep an eye on the clock. A hungry toddler is often a cranky, uncooperative toddler. Some of our family's biggest food battles have happened after the kids have gone *a little* too long between meals. (And then they don't eat, even though food is the only thing that will help them feel better, and the fussing goes on much longer than it should.)

Once a meal begins, toddlers have a limited attention span for eating. After their initial hunger is satisfied, giving them too long at the table often results in them finding messy ways to entertain themselves. (Even now, one of Jennifer's kids will sit at the table picking at food for *hours* if given the chance.) Creating a general, flexible schedule with set beginning and end times for meals and snacks will make things easier on all of you in the long run.

Be prepared for your toddler to have big swings in eating habits. It's strange—sometimes your toddler can literally out-eat you; other times, it seems like your toddler exists on nothing but air and crackers. These swings can be unsettling, but they're normal toddler behavior. Generally, their eating evens out over the course of a few days or weeks. Talk to your pediatrician if you're worried about weight or nutrition, but if your pediatrician is happy, your toddler is good to go. To reduce waste, we generally serve very small portions to toddlers and let them ask for seconds (and thirds) if they're hungry.

Also, don't expect toddlers to be consistent with their food preferences! Toddlers can be irrationally obsessed with a food one week and reject it the next. It's frustrating ("But just five minutes ago you *asked* me to cook you this!?"), but it's normal life with toddlers.

For younger toddlers, we've had good luck with pairing new foods with favorite foods, serving multiple healthy side dishes at mealtimes, and letting them feed themselves regardless of the mess. For older toddlers, offering choices of foods before cooking helps feed their need for independence and makes them more willing to eat what you've cooked.

Make mealtimes playful family time. When possible, sit down for meals with your toddler. Sharing meals is a great time for connection, and it gives you the chance to model healthy eating habits. (It also allows you to keep an eye on the mess and intervene before it gets out of hand.)

We've also found that kids eat best when there's an element of fun involved. Those same "airplane noise" games that worked for your babies can be adjusted to work for your toddler. Games we've had good luck with include the following:

- Have your toddler "steal" their food from you. For this one, you bring your chair up close to the toddler's chair and scoop a bite up off their plate. Say something like, "Look, I'm going to eat this delicious bite of broccoli!" and then pretend you're raising the food to your mouth while actually putting it in front of your toddler. If your toddler is into the game, they'll lean in and take "your" bite off the spoon, then you look around for the food.

- Pretend your toddler is an animal and the food is their animal food. This game is easily modified to match their current obsession (like construction trucks eating gas and oil or princesses eating royal food).

- Ask the toddler to take different size bites. ("Show me a grandma bite, a baby bite, a shark bite," and so on.)

- Reverse roles by having your toddler try to feed you a bite of something and you pretend not to like it. Make it clear you're being silly, bring in elements of their behavior when they refuse to try something, and encourage them to be the parent trying to get you to eat. Let the toddler "convince" you to put the food in your mouth and make a big deal of stopping your fuss and changing your mind to liking the food. (This game works best for older toddlers.)

Keep in mind that some toddlers will respond better to some games than others and that the games that work well for one kid may not work for another. However, introducing play into mealtime can significantly help your toddler stay interested in the meal and help them be more willing to try new foods. Find what works for you!

Prepare for picky phases. Some kids are easygoing eaters; others . . . not so much. However, over time, you'll find that each kid also swings in their own range, so even an easygoing eater will have picky periods where a once-favorite food is no longer acceptable. Don't be offended—it's not you, it's them.

In our experience, pickiness comes from two places: genuine uncertainty about or dislike of certain flavors/textures and a need to exert control. For the first issue, we've found that it works well to acknowledge a food is unfamiliar or isn't a favorite and involve them in figuring out if there's a way they can make the food work for them.

As far as control is concerned, let's face it: no matter how convenient it would be, you can't *make* your toddler eat. While as a parent you have a few power plays, like punishing (not a great option because it turns mealtimes into regular power struggles) or bribing (also not great because it makes every mealtime an exhausting negotiation on the number of bites), the most effective long-term solution is finding positive ways to encourage your toddler to eat.

In addition to the games mentioned previously, we've had great luck in "rebranding" foods by riffing on the name of a favorite food. For instance, a toddler may swear they hate pasta with pesto sauce, but they'll *love* eating green mac and cheese (aka pesto with a little mozzarella on top). So, you might consider serving green mac, toma-to mac (regular spaghetti sauce), and cheese mac (actual macaroni and cheese) and see what happens.

Let others step in. With toddlers, there will be times where they just won't eat for you, no matter what foods you serve or games you try. It can be particularly maddening to deal with this pushback day after day (after day), and you might be exasperated enough to try bribing or punishing. In these instances, call on your support squad! Ask a trusted friend or relative to feed your child for a meal or two as needed. Sometimes, Grandma or a favorite uncle has the magic touch, and your toddler will happily eat things for them that they'd never eat for you. So, let them step in while you enjoy a meal in peace! Sometimes time away is just as important for the toddler as it is for the parent.

Go-to Phrases to Help Take the Battles Out of Eating

We've all had moments where absolutely nothing could convince our kids to eat a certain food. However, we've stumbled on the following phrases that have helped us—maybe they can be a starting point for you and your family. (These work best with older toddlers.)

"It's not my taste."
There's nothing like the feeling of being over to dinner at someone's house and having your toddler yell "YUCKY!" at full volume. Around our dinner table, we've had lots of conversations about how different people like different foods and so certain foods aren't inherently "yucky" or "yummy." We bring up their favorite foods and the people they know who don't like those foods. Toddlers also really enjoy it when they like a food that's not Mom or Dad's taste.

Eventually, they understand that if they don't like a certain food, it just isn't their taste at the moment—*and that's OK!* For us, this has reduced power struggles around eating and has also led to less fussing when we cook one of their less-favorite meals.

"You don't have to like it, you just have to try it to see if your tastes have changed."
Usually, we have a pretty good idea if our children will like a meal. For the foods you suspect will be met with resistance, try to have a few sides on the table you know they'll like—favorite fruits, vegetables, breads, or crackers. Give your toddler a very small serving of everything on the table and emphasize that you aren't sure whether their tastes have changed, so you'd like them to try just one good bite.

Generally, the kids take a bite and leave the rest on their plate. If they've done one good bite, let them fill up on the side dishes they enjoy. Occasionally, though, there's an excited, "Mom, my tastes have changed!" When that happens, really celebrate and talk about how much they're growing up.

"How can we make it more your taste?"
Occasionally, you'll be caught off-guard when your toddler declares something is not their taste—especially when the meal has ingredients they like or when it was a meal they used to ask for often. In those instances, when you don't have other options on the table, ask your toddler to think of ideas that would help make the meal more to their liking.

Let your children know that you don't make separate meals for kids and parents in your house. However, also let them know that you are willing to try simple, no-cook things to modify the meal, like turning salads into sandwiches, serving sauces on the side, picking out certain ingredients (after trying one), cutting it into different shapes, or adding ingredients to their foods. Usually, adding ingredients consists of adding salt, pepper, butter, or ketchup, but occasionally, they'll ask for off-the-wall toppings like sour cream on breakfast foods or sprinkles on a baked potato. In those instances, let them try a bite with a small amount of the desired topping on it first and let them add more if they still want to.

Giving your child control of how to modify a meal can cut down on mealtime battles because it puts you on the same team looking for a solution you can both live with.

Pressure Cooking Essentials

Using Your Pressure Cooker

The recipes in this cookbook are written to work in all brands of electric pressure cookers, including the Instant Pot. While you may already be familiar with the pressure cooking terminology and settings for your specific device, for your convenience, we've included a brief guide explaining how we've used these terms in this cookbook.

Pressure Cooker Parts

It might look complicated initially, but your electric pressure cooker is actually pretty simple when you get to know it, and all brands have similar components. For questions specific to your particular model, check your user manual.

Housing. This is the outer part of the pressure cooker that contains the buttons and the heating element and is connected to the cord. *DO NOT add ingredients directly to the housing or you may permanently damage your pressure cooker.*

Cooking Pot. This is the inner removable pot, and it's where the magic happens. While you're adding the ingredients to this pot, treat the cooking pot like you treat any pot on the stove—for example, lifting it up off the heating element to slow the cooking. Once you lock the lid in place, however, you'll be unable to access this pot until the pressure is released.

Sealing Ring. This large flexible ring attaches to the underside of the lid. When the lid is locked, the sealing ring prevents steam from escaping, allowing the machine to build pressure inside the pot.

Float Valve and Mini Gasket. This small valve fits inside the lid and is paired with a miniature silicone gasket. When your machine reaches pressure, steam pushes the float valve up and seals the pressure cooker, locking the lid until the float valve drops again, indicating pressure inside the cooker has been released.

Pressure Release Switch. This piece is located on the lid and controls how the pressure inside the pot can escape. In one position, it will seal the steam inside your electric pressure cooker, and in another, it will allow the steam to release quickly. (Depending on your model of electric pressure cooker, this may be called a *switch, valve*, or *button*, but the function is identical.)

Cook Settings

While each model of pressure cooker has different buttons and different functions, most of them are just preset cook times for different foods. *Remember, your pressure cooker CANNOT actually sense what you are cooking and CANNOT tell you when the food in your pot is cooked through.* Since the recipes in this cookbook were developed for all brands of electric pressure cookers, we avoid the preset buttons and use only the following settings:

High Pressure/Manual/Pressure Cook. This setting tells the machine to cook at high pressure. When a recipe says, "Select High Pressure and 5 minutes cook time," this will be the setting you use. (The exact name of this setting will depend on the model of electric pressure cooker you own. If your model of pressure cooker doesn't have a manual setting, consult your user guide and choose the preset button with the closest time to the time in the recipe.)

Sauté/Simmer/Browning. This setting allows you to use the cooking pot like any other stovetop pot. Use this setting with the lid off. (Depending on your brand of electric pressure cooker, you may have separate buttons for each heat level or a single button that can adjust the heat level up or down as desired. Some brands don't have a Sauté button, and users select a preset button with the lid off.)

Keep Warm. When the cook time ends, many electric pressure cookers will automatically switch to the Keep Warm setting. Be aware that the contents of your pan will continue to cook as long as this setting is on. This setting can be useful; however, we recommend turning this setting off or unplugging the pressure cooker if you're prone to forgetting to remove the cooking pot from the housing once the meal is complete. And, of course, be sure to turn off your pressure cooker when you're done using it.

Pressure Release Methods

After the cook time has ended, the timer will sound. At this point, the recipe will direct you to release the pressure using the following methods:

Quick Pressure Release. When the cook time ends, turn the pressure release switch to Venting and watch the pressure cooker release a jet of steam. Be sure to position your pressure cooker so that the steam vents away from your cabinets and avoid placing your face or hands directly over the vent, as the steam can burn. If liquid or foam starts coming out of the vent, return the switch to the Sealed position for a minute or two, then try venting the pressure again. Wait until the pressure is completely released, the float valve drops, and the lid unlocks easily before trying to remove the lid.

Natural Pressure Release. When the cook time ends, just leave the pressure release switch in the Sealed position. The pressure will release slowly through the switch, with no visible jet of steam or noise. With this method, the only way you'll know the pressure is fully released is the float valve will drop and the lid will unlock easily. (It's a bit anticlimactic in comparison.)

Many recipes combine these release methods, instructing you to allow the pressure to release naturally for a certain amount of time, then finish with a quick pressure release. To do this, simply wait the specified number of minutes and then turn the switch from Sealed to Venting to release any remaining pressure.

Pressure Cooking Accessories

A few simple accessories will make cooking a little easier and will help you get even more time savings from your pressure cooker. Some of these items will come with your pressure cooker, and you may already own other accessories that can be used in your pressure cooker. Generally, as long as it's an oven-safe dish that fits on a trivet inside the inner cooking pot with room for steam to rise around the dish, it's good to go.

The following accessories are ones we've used in this cookbook; however, you don't need all of these all at once. If you're thinking of purchasing some accessories, we recommend starting with an instant-read thermometer, for food safety, and a round cake pan and trivet, since many of our recipes use the pot-in-pot cooking method. Add the other accessories as your budget allows.

Compartmentalized serving dishes. Whether you use an ice cube tray, divided plates, or the silicone baby food containers mentioned below, consider getting a dish with small compartments that will allow you to put different foods in each compartment, allowing your toddler to have some control over what they eat and how they eat it.

Double-stack pot. This accessory is newer to the pressure cooking world; essentially, it's a set of stackable pans where the top pan works as a lid to the bottom pan and fits perfectly inside the pressure cooking pot. This pot gives you a little more freedom for pot-in-pot cooking.

Extra silicone ring. Because the silicone ring sometimes takes on the smell of your most recent meal, we prefer to have at least two silicone rings for our pressure cooker: one for savory, spicy, or strong-smelling foods and another for breakfasts, fruits, and desserts.

Half-size Bundt pan. A half-size (6-cup [1.4 L]) Bundt pan without a large rim fits perfectly in a 6-quart (5.7 L) pressure cooker. This pan allows foods like the Blueberries and Cream Baked French Toast (page 48) to cook more quickly and evenly than they would in a simple cake pan.

Immersion blender. While any blender works with these recipes, an immersion blender lets you blend directly in a wide-mouth mason jar or pressure cooking pot without having to worry about spilling or waste from transferring to a separate blender. (If you have a nonstick cooking pot, be careful not to scratch your pot with an immersion blender.)

Instant-read thermometer. Whether it's a fork-style or pen-style thermometer, this important food-safety tool helps you ensure that foods have reached a safe internal temperature. Because cuts of meat can vary widely in size and thickness, it is always wise to check meats for doneness. Common safe internal temperatures are as follows:

Breads and cakes	210°F (99 °C)
Baked potatoes	205°F (96 °C)
Chicken thighs and wings	180°F (82 °C)
Beef (well-done)	165°F (74 °C)
Chicken breasts	165°F (74 °C)
Ground beef	155°F (68 °C)

Kitchen shears. While this kitchen gadget isn't pressure cooker–specific, it is by far our most-used tool for feeding toddlers. Whether you call them "shears" or "scissors," these sharp, oversized scissors make it a snap to snip meats, veggies, and breads into toddler-friendly bites.

Mason jars. Wide-mouth mason jars are the perfect size to fit an immersion blender. You can fit up to four tall pint-size (473 ml)-size wide-mouth mason jars in a 6-quart (5.7 L) pressure cooker, allowing you to cook multiple foods at the same time. (Be aware that common brands make two shapes of pint-size (473 ml)-size wide-mouth mason jars—short and tall—and only the tall ones fit four at once.)

Retriever tongs. Many people prefer to use these little grabbers to remove the inner pan from the pressure cooking pot when doing pot-in-pot cooking.

Round cake pan. A 7 x 3-inch (18 x 7.5 cm) round cake pan is a pressure cooking must! It's the secret for pot-in-pot cooking, which allows you to cook sides and sauces at the same time you cook your meal.

Silicone baby food containers. These flexible containers are perfect for making mini muffins and egg bites. The recipes in this book are developed for an 8-inch (20 cm) tray with seven cups. The flexible silicone makes it easy to remove the cooked foods from the cups with a gentle push on the bottom of the cup.

Silicone mini mitts. These inexpensive, flexible mitts work like hot pads but give you more grip and control when handling a hot pressure cooking pot—and the all-silicone design is extra easy to clean.

Sling. A sling makes it much easier to remove hot pans from the cooking pot when doing pot-in-pot cooking. You can make your own sling out of a long strip of aluminum foil folded into thirds so it's about 26 inches (65 cm) long by 4 inches (10 cm) wide.

Springform pan. We recommend a leakproof 7-inch (18 cm) spring-form pan for making foods that may be hard to remove from a cake pan, such as our Alex'sBrownie Pops (page 106).

Steamer basket. A steamer basket keeps foods out of the water and has small holes like a colander. This tool is really useful for cooking foods that break down easily in water and makes them easy to remove from the pressure cooking pot.

Trivet. A trivet (sometimes called a *rack*) keeps ingredients and pots off of the bottom of the pressure cooking pot. Because they are relatively inexpensive, we prefer to have two: a short trivet (½ inch [1.3 cm] or less) for taller cooking accessories like mason jars and a tall trivet (2 to 3 inches [5 to 7.5 cm] high) for cooking side dishes and sauces over a main dish.

Tips, Tricks, and Troubleshooting

Life with toddlers is busy enough—the last thing you need is to spend time running to the store in the middle of cooking or fixing a meal that didn't work out. Here are a few tips and tricks that will help you get started.

Know your model size. The recipes in this cookbook were created in and tested using a 6-quart (5.7 L) electric pressure cooker. While these recipes will work in larger pressure cookers, your cook time may be slightly different, and you may need to use more liquid than the recipe calls for. Many of the recipes will also work in smaller pressure cookers; however, the pot-in-pot recipes may need to be cooked separately.

Read the whole recipe before you start cooking. This is a simple thing that has a huge effect on your cooking (and your stress level while cooking)! Reading though the recipe ensures you're familiar with the timing and ingredients, accounts for any resting time, and helps reduce errors. Also, many recipes have serving suggestions at the end, so reading ahead helps you plan when you need to start these items so they'll be ready when you need them.

Prepare your ingredients before cooking. It's frustrating to get halfway through a recipe and realize you're missing a key ingredient. By having your ingredients measured and chopped before you start cooking, you'll be ready for quick transitions and the actual cooking process will go more smoothly.

Trust your senses. Listen to your intuition and don't doubt what you see and smell! For example, if the recipe calls for more time, but the food you're cooking looks and smells done, then move on to the next step. If the food looks or smells like it's cooking too quickly, take the cooking pot out of the housing or add the liquid to the pot.

Check the temperature of your meat. Due to variations in size and thickness of the meat, sometimes the meat in your pot will need a little longer cook time than the recipe suggests. As soon as you've released the pressure, you'll want to check the meat for doneness, consulting the temperature guidelines on page 27.

Grease your pans generously. When you spray your pans with nonstick cooking or baking spray, make sure you're using enough to coat the pans well and that you're spreading it around well with a paper towel, distributing the spray along any corners or creases. (This is especially important with the silicone pans, where foods are more likely to stick.)

Get familiar with pot-in-pot cooking. When you're cooking pot-in-pot, some foods may take a little longer to cook because they're a little farther from the heating element. (For example, we've found white rice does better with 4 minutes pot-in-pot, compared to 3 minutes when cooked the traditional way.) If something you've cooked pot-in-pot isn't done to your liking, make a note to add another minute or two the next time you make it. Also, if you're steaming something pot-in-pot, try to get in the habit of adding the water to the pot *before* you put the trivet or steamer basket in the cooking pot—just to make sure you don't forget it!

Cook a double batch of favorite recipes. Many of these recipes are easily doubled in a standard 6-quart (5.7 L) pressure cooker without increasing the cook time. However, be aware that if you're doubling a main dish, it may be too much volume to cook the side dish pot-in-pot at the same time.

Follow food safety practices. This includes basics like washing your hands well, keeping raw meats away from other food prep, and thawing food in the refrigerator or in cold water. Cooked food must be refrigerated or frozen within 2 hours or discarded, and the sooner you can get leftovers in the fridge, the better. Once refrigerated, be sure to use or freeze according to USDA or common food standards. (And, of course, use your judgment—when in doubt, throw it out!)

Cooked Toddler Food	Refrigerator	Freezer
Baked goods (muffins, brownies)	3 to 5 days	2 to 3 months
Beef	3 to 4 days	2 to 3 months*
Chicken	3 to 4 days	2 to 3 months*
Cut fruits	3 to 4 days	1 to 2 months
Fruit sauces (compotes)	Up to 7 days	2 to 3 months
Pasta	3 to 5 days	1 to 2 months
Pork	3 to 4 days	2 to 3 months*
Potatoes	3 to 4 days	1 to 2 months
Rice	4 to 6 days	4 to 6 months
Soups	3 to 4 days	2 to 3 months
Vegetables	3 to 4 days	1 to 2 months

* If meats are covered in gravy or broth, they can be stored in the freezer for up to 6 months.

Solutions to Common Concerns

Once in a while, something goes wrong as you're cooking—it even happens to cooks who aren't distracted by toddlers! For brand-specific troubleshooting tips, consult your pressure cooker user manual; however, for your convenience, we've included our solutions to the most common concerns we hear from blog readers, family, and friends.

Steam is coming from my pressure cooker. First, determine where the steam is coming from. If it's coming from the pressure release switch or the float valve, double-check that the pressure release switch is fully in place and turned to the Sealed position. If it's from the float valve, use a quick pressure release, remove the lid, then check that the float valve is properly installed and that the mini gasket is tightly in place. If steam is escaping from the sides of the lid, and use a quick pressure release and check that the silicone sealing ring is tightly in place around the entire lid. In rare cases, the sealing ring is cracked or broken; in this case, unfortunately, the only solution is to replace it.

If you notice the steam escaping early in the cooking process, you can simply restart the High Pressure cook time. However, if a number of minutes went by before you noticed the problem, you may need to add more liquid to the cooking pot and reduce the cook time—there's no hard rule for how much, just make your best guess.

My pressure cooker sprays liquid when releasing the steam.
This can happen, especially when you're cooking starchy foods like grains, dried beans, or pastas. If water starts to spray during your quick pressure release, return the pressure release switch to the Sealed position. Wait 30 seconds, then open the pressure release switch again and allow pressure to release. If more liquid comes out, repeat the process. With some foods, one or two closed intervals is all you need before you can leave the switch in the Venting position; with other foods, it takes several closed intervals to fully release the pressure.

My food scorched while using the Sauté setting. Be aware that the sauté times in the recipes are guidelines; due to differences in thickness and sizes of meats and vegetables, your food may need more or less time. If your food needs less time browning, simply add the premeasured liquid called for in the recipes (often broth or water). If your food needs additional time browning, simply add another tablespoon (15 ml) of oil or butter and continue the cooking process.

Also, just like a pot on an electric stovetop, you can also lift the cooking pot away from the heating element in the housing to slow the cooking process. If possible, adjust your pressure cooker to sauté on a lower heat setting. (If your pressure cooker does not adjust to low, consider browning in a separate pot on the stove.) Finally, if you're cooking pot-in-pot, make sure the inside pot is resting on a trivet above liquids and not directly on the pressure cooking pot.

My food isn't cooked through. If your food is nearly done, select Sauté and finish cooking the dish on that setting for a few minutes. However, if your meat isn't close to the proper temperature or isn't as fall-apart tender as you'd like, lock the lid in place, cook for a few additional minutes at High Pressure, and then use the pressure release called for in the recipe. If quicker-cooking foods like vegetables or rice are done but your meat is not, if possible, remove these ingredients from the cooking pot and cover them with aluminum foil before returning the meat to High Pressure.

If this happens when you're "baking" foods in the pressure cooker, make sure you've followed the instructions on whether to bake covered or uncovered, because covering the pan with foil has a big effect on the total cook time.

My food stuck to the pan. If you're cooking pot-in-pot, spray your inner pan generously with nonstick cooking spray or baking spray with flour and use a paper towel to ensure the entire pan is coated. Let your food cool in the pan for at least 5 minutes before trying to remove it; if necessary, run a thin spatula around the edges of the pan to help separate it.

If your food stuck to the pressure cooking pot, make sure that you added enough liquid and that it was evenly distributed on the bottom of the cooking pot. Since the bottom of the cooking pot is slightly domed, the melted butter and oil tend to run to the sides—in these instances, tilt the cooking pot so that the oil covers the entire surface. Finally, remember that larger 8- and 10-quart (7.2 to 9.5 L) cookers may need more liquid than their smaller 6-quart (5.4 L) counterparts.

My soup/sauce/compote/oatmeal/risotto turned out too thin. When these foods come out of the pressure cooker too thin, there's usually an easy fix. First, give the ingredients a good stir to ensure that the liquid hasn't settled on the top. Next, remember that these foods thicken as they cool, so if they're close to your desired thickness, remove the cooking pot from the housing, allow to cool uncovered for 5 minutes, then check the thickness again. If there's much more liquid than desired, select Sauté and cook, stirring constantly, until the food reaches the desired thickness.

If you're in a hurry, you can also add a thickener to soups, sauces, and compotes. In a small bowl, stir together 1 tablespoon (8 g) cornstarch and 1 tablespoon (15 ml) cold water and slowly add the slurry to the cooking pot, stirring constantly. Select Sauté and stir until the food reaches a boiling point, which will activate the thickening agents in the cornstarch. (When in doubt, take a lighter hand on the thickener because too much can create a gelatin effect.)

My soup/sauce/compote/oatmeal/risotto turned out too thick.
If your foods come out of the pressure cooker too thick, you'll need to give them a good stir to ensure nothing has scorched on the bottom. If not, simply add more of the main liquid in the recipe (e.g., water, broth, cream, juice, or almond milk) and stir until well combined. You'll often need to add a good amount of liquids when reheating leftovers, because these foods thicken significantly as they cool.

My food isn't sweet/spicy/flavorful enough. Keep in mind that these recipes were designed for the toddler palate and that adults are welcome to add favorite seasonings or extra sugar to adjust the meal to their individual palates. Also, for meals that call for fruits, there can be a big variation in the sweetness and ripeness of the fruits, so you'll want to taste it before cooking. If the fruit is very tart, add a little sugar or juice before cooking.

My silicone ring still smells like yesterday's dinner. Unfortunately, the food-grade silicone that allows pressure cookers to come to pressure also has a tendency to take on the smells of the foods being cooked—we haven't yet come across a brand of pressure cooker that doesn't have this problem. For the most part, the odor will not impact the food you're cooking.

Although there are dozens of methods that try to remove food smells from the silicone ring—soaking or steaming in lemon juice, vinegar, coffee grounds, tomato juice, and even bleach—we haven't found one that completely gets rid of the smell. To minimize the smell, we prefer to store the silicone rings so they have a chance to air out and to have one ring for savory meats and another for mild breakfast foods and desserts.

CHAPTER 1

BREAKFASTS

Start the day off with a variety of sweet and savory meals that both you and your toddler will love. Many of these recipes can be made ahead and warmed up in the morning when you and your toddler are ready to start the day.

EVAN'S LEMON BERRY BREAKFAST RISOTTO

Jennifer's son is proud to have helped create this recipe—he listed the ingredients he'd like (all his favorite flavors)—and we love how it turned out. He likes to go heavy on the berries, so we generally dice double the berries called for here. Makes 4 servings.

2 tablespoons (28 g) unsalted butter

1½ cups (270 g) Arborio rice

4 cups (946 ml) unsweetened almond milk, plus more for serving

2-4 tablespoons (26 to 50 g) sugar

zest of 1 lemon

1 tablespoon (15 ml) lemon juice

1 teaspoon vanillla extract, optional

¼ teaspoon salt

1½ cups diced (255 g)strawberries, (190 g) raspberries, (220 g) blackberries, or (220 g) blueberries, for serving

1. Select Sauté and melt the butter in the pressure cooking pot. Stir in the rice and cook for 3 to 4 minutes, stirring frequently, until the rice becomes opaque. Stir in the almond milk, sugar, lemon zest, lemon juice, vanilla, and salt. Lock the lid in place. Select High Pressure and 6 minutes cook time.

2. When the cook time ends, turn off the pressure cooker. Let the pressure release naturally for 5 minutes, then finish with a quick pressure release. When the float valve drops, carefully remove the lid.

3. Remove the cooking pot from the housing. Stir the risotto to mix in any liquid that may have settled on the top. (The mixture will continue to thicken as it cools; however, if there's more liquid than you like, select Sauté and cook to the desired consistency.)

4. Serve topped with diced fresh berries and a splash of almond milk.

TIP

We love the flavor and texture that almond milk gives this dish; however, if you wish, you can substitute 1 cup (235 ml) heavy cream or half-and-half and 3 cups (700 ml) water for the almond milk. Don't substitute milk in a 1:1 ratio because the lemon juice can cause the milk to curdle slightly while cooking.

BANANA CREAM
BREAKFAST RISOTTO

Most kids love bananas, and your family will go bananas for this smooth, creamy breakfast risotto. It's a fun way to start the day! Makes 4 servings.

2 tablespoons (28 g) unsalted butter

1½ cups (270 g) Arborio rice

3 cups (700 ml) water

1 cup (235 ml) heavy cream, plus more for serving

1 tablespoon (14 g) brown sugar, plus more for serving

1 teaspoon vanilla extract

¼ teaspoon salt

2 to 4 ounces (55 to 115 g) cream cheese, at room temperature, cubed

1 fresh banana, well mashed

1 to 2 fresh bananas, thinly sliced

Whipped cream for serving, optional

1. Select Sauté and melt the butter in the pressure cooking pot. Stir in the rice and cook for 3 to 4 minutes, stirring frequently, until the rice becomes opaque. Stir in the water, heavy cream, brown sugar, vanilla, and salt. Lock the lid in place. Select High Pressure and 6 minutes cook time.

2. When the cook time ends, turn off the pressure cooker. Let the pressure release naturally for 5 minutes, then finish with a quick pressure release. When the float valve drops, carefully remove the lid.

3. Remove the cooking pot from the housing. Stir the risotto to mix in any liquid that may have settled on the top. (The mixture will continue to thicken as it cools.) Stir in the cream cheese and mashed banana.

4. Serve topped with fresh banana slices, a sprinkle of brown sugar (if desired), and a splash of cream or a dollop of whipped cream, if desired.

TIP

If you're dishing up individual servings each day, only slice as much fresh banana as you need and add the fresh banana after reheating. To reheat, stir in additional cream, milk, or water, and microwave on 50 percent power until the risotto reaches the desired temperature.

FRUIT COCKTAIL STEEL CUT OATS

Colorful fruit cocktail is generally less expensive than fresh fruit and is available year-round. Feel better about serving this kid favorite by using it as a topping for some hearty, long-lasting oats.

Makes 4 servings.

1 tablespoon (14 g) unsalted butter

1 cup (80 g) steel cut oats

2¼ cups (550 ml) water

½ cup (120 ml) heavy cream

1 teaspoon vanilla extract

⅛ teaspoon salt

1 can (15 ounces, or 425 g) or 4 containers (4 ounces, or 115 g each) of fruit cocktail in water or 100% juice

1. Select Sauté and melt the butter in the pressure cooking pot. Add the oats. Toast for about 3 minutes, stirring constantly, until they smell nutty. Stir in the water, heavy cream, vanilla, and salt. Lock the lid in place. Select High Pressure and 10 minutes cook time.

2. While the oats cook, strain the fruit cocktail over a cup, reserving the juice.

3. When the cook time ends, turn off the pressure cooker. Let the pressure release naturally for 10 minutes, then finish with a quick pressure release. When the float valve drops, carefully remove the lid. Stir the cooked oats in the pressure cooking pot. (They will be quite thick.) Add the drained fruit and enough reserved juice to bring the oats to the desired consistency. Stir to combine. These oats get thicker as they cool; if the consistency becomes thicker than desired, stir in additional reserved fruit juice, heavy cream, or water as needed.

TIP

If you're dishing up individual servings each day, one 4-ounce (115 g) container of fruit cocktail is about the right amount for 1 serving of steel cut oats. You may still want to reserve some of the juice because thicker oats will be easier for toddlers to eat. To reheat, stir in additional reserved fruit juice, cream, or water and microwave on 50 percent power until the oats reach the desired temperature.

RAINBOW FRUIT YOGURT PARFAITS

These parfaits are a colorful, delicious start to the day! This easy recipe allows you to make four different fruit compotes at the same time—and you can blend them and store them in the same jars they cook in! Makes 4 servings.

Red Raspberry-Strawberry Compote

½ cup raspberries, (65 g) fresh or (70 g) frozen

½ cup strawberries, (73 g) fresh or (75 g) frozen

1 tablespoon (15 ml) apple juice

Yellow Peach Compote

1 cup (154 g) diced yellow peaches, (154 g) fresh or (140 g) frozen

1 tablespoon (15 ml) apple juice

Green Pineapple Compote

1 cup (165 g) chopped fresh pineapple

¾ cup (23 g) baby spinach leaves

1 tablespoon (15 ml) apple juice

Blueberry Compote

½ cup blueberries, (75 g) fresh or (78 g) frozen

½ cup blackberries, (75 g) fresh or (75 g) frozen

1 tablespoon (15 ml) apple juice

1 cup (235 ml) water

2 tablespoons (16 g) cornstarch, optional

2 tablespoons (28 ml) cold water, optional

1 pint (473 g) Greek store-bought or homemade yogurt, plain or vanilla flavor

Additional fresh fruit, for serving, optional

1. *Prepare the compotes:* In four separate wide-mouth pint (473 ml)-size mason jars, prepare the raspberry-strawberry, peach, pineapple, and blueberry compotes by combining the ingredients in each jar. Do not place lids on the mason jars.

2. Add 1 cup (235 ml) water to the pressure cooking pot. Add a trivet to the pot and place the mason jars on top. Lock the lid in place. Select High Pressure and 2 minutes cook time.

3. When the cook time ends, turn off the pressure cooker. Let the pressure release naturally for 10 minutes, then finish with a quick pressure release. When the float valve drops, carefully remove the lid.

4. Remove the mason jars from the pressure cooking pot. Use an immersion blender directly in the mason jar to blend the compotes to the desired consistency. The compotes will thicken as they cool.

5. If you'd like a thicker compote, in a small bowl, stir together cornstarch and 2 tablespoons (28 ml) cold water until well combined. Divide the slurry evenly among the four jars. Return the mason jars to the pressure cooker and select High Pressure and 0 minutes cook time. Remove mason jars and cool to room temperature, then refrigerate until ready to serve.

6. To serve, in a cup, layer a spoonful of yogurt, then a spoonful of the blueberry compote, then yogurt, and repeat with the green, yellow, and red compotes. Top with additional diced fresh fruit, if desired.

TIP

The wide-mouth pint (473 ml)-size mason jars come in two different shapes—wide and tall. You'll need the tall ones if you want to fit all four jars in a 6-quart (5.7 L) pressure cooker. You can find these jars in most big-box stores, some grocery stores, or online.

BLUEBERRIES AND CREAM
BAKED FRENCH TOAST

Serving fun, indulgent breakfasts on the weekends is a tradition your kids are sure to remember. This French toast might just become a weekend breakfast staple in your house—the rich lemon cream is easy to make and is a great alternative to maple syrup.

Makes 4 servings.

Lemon Cream

4 ounces (115 g) cream cheese, at room temperature

2 tablespoons (40 g) lemon curd

1 tablespoon (13 g) sugar

½ cup (120 ml) heavy cream

½ teaspoon vanilla extract

Blueberry French Toast

Nonstick baking spray with flour

4 tablespoons (55 g) butter, melted

¼ cup (50 g) sugar

2 cups (475 ml) whole milk

3 eggs, beaten

1 teaspoon vanilla extract

¼ teaspoon salt

10 cups (500 g) cubed challah bread (about 1 loaf)

½ cup (75 g) fresh blueberries

1 cup (235 ml) water

1. *Prepare the Lemon Cream:* Using a handheld mixer, in a small bowl, beat the cream cheese, lemon curd, and 1 tablespoon (13 g) sugar until smooth. Add the heavy cream and vanilla and beat until soft peaks form. Refrigerate until ready to serve. (We prefer to make this the night before.)

2. *Prepare the French Toast:* Generously coat a 7-inch (18 cm) cake pan with nonstick baking spray with flour. In a large bowl, whisk together the melted butter and ¼ cup (50 g) sugar. Add the milk, beaten eggs, vanilla, and salt. Mix in the cubed bread. Let rest until the bread absorbs the milk, stirring occasionally. Gently stir in the fresh blueberries. Gently press the bread mixture into the prepared pan.

3. Pour 1 cup (235 ml) water into the pressure cooking pot and place a trivet in the bottom. Carefully center the filled pan on a sling and lower the pan onto the trivet. Lock the lid in place. Select High Pressure and 25 minutes cook time.

4. When the cook time ends, turn off the pressure cooker. Let the pressure release naturally for 5 minutes, then finish with a quick pressure release. When the float valve drops, carefully remove the lid. Use the sling to transfer the pan to a wire rack.

5. If desired, put the dish under a preheated broiler to crisp the top. Cut into slices and serve topped with a dollop of the Lemon Cream.

TIP

The type of bread you use makes a big difference in how your baked French toast turns out. If you can't find challah bread, you can substitute another rich bread like brioche, Hawaiian sweet bread, or croissants. Other types of bread won't absorb as much liquid when cooked, so if you use a different type of bread, you'll need to reduce your liquids accordingly.

BANANA BREAD BITES

These fun-to-eat banana bread bites are the perfect size for little hands. Banana bread is a moist, dense bread that is perfect for cooking in the pressure cooker. Makes 14 bites.

Nonstick baking spray with flour

1½ cups (188 g) all-purpose flour

1 teaspoon baking powder

¼ teaspoon baking soda

¼ teaspoon salt

1 cup (225 g) mashed very ripe banana (about 3 small)

⅓ cup (75 g) brown sugar

¼ cup (60 g) sour cream

3 tablespoons (42 g) unsalted butter, melted

½ teaspoon vanilla extract

1 large egg, beaten

¼ cup (28 g) chopped toasted pecans, (30g) walnuts, or (28 g) slivered almonds, optional

¼ cup (30 g) dried cranberries, optional

1 cup (235 ml) water

1. Spray two silicone baby food trays with nonstick baking spray with flour. In a small bowl, sift together the flour, baking powder, baking soda, and salt. Set aside.

2. In a large bowl, combine the mashed bananas, brown sugar, sour cream, butter, and vanilla. Add the egg and using a handheld electric mixer, beat at medium speed until well blended.

3. Fold in the dry ingredients, then gently mix in the nuts and cranberries, if using. Stir until just blended. Evenly divide the batter among the silicone cups; do not fill more than two-thirds full. Place a paper towel on top of the silicone tray and cover with aluminum foil.

4. Pour 1 cup (235 ml) water into the pressure cooking pot and place a trivet in the bottom. Use a sling to carefully lower the silicone trays into the pot, stacking one tray on top of the other. Lock the lid in place. Select High Pressure and 25 minutes cook time.

5. When the cook time ends, turn off the pressure cooker. Let the pressure release naturally for 5 minutes, then finish with a quick pressure release. When the float valve drops, carefully remove the lid and use the sling to remove the trays. Place on a wire rack and remove the foil and paper towel. Allow to cool for 10 minutes, then turn the cups over and gently squeeze to remove the muffins from the trays.

TIP

This banana bread recipe has been in the family for decades. It's a forgiving recipe; you can make substitutions based on what you have on hand: Greek yogurt for sour cream, margarine for butter, or even increase or decrease the sugar content. Play around with it and see what works best for your family!

BLUEBERRY MUFFIN BITES

Did you know you can "bake" in the pressure cooker? These light and fluffy muffins start with a muffin mix, so they're perfect when you need something quick and easy to put together. Makes 7 bites.

Nonstick baking spray with flour

1 box (7 ounces or 200 g) blueberry muffin mix, prepared according to package directions

¼ cup (36 g) fresh blueberries

1 cup (235 ml) water

1. Generously coat one silicone baby food tray with nonstick baking spray with flour. In a small bowl, prepare the blueberry muffin mix. Set aside.

2. Place half of the muffin batter in the silicone tray, then distribute half of the blueberries evenly among the cups. Repeat with the remaining batter and blueberries. Do not fill the cups more than half full.

3. Place a paper towel on top of the silicone tray and cover tightly with aluminum foil.

4. Pour 1 cup (235 ml) water into the pressure cooking pot and place a trivet in the bottom. Use a sling to carefully lower the silicone tray into the pot. Lock the lid in place. Select High Pressure and 12 minutes cook time.

5. When the cook time ends, turn off the pressure cooker. Let the pressure release naturally for 5 minutes, then finish with a quick pressure release. When the float valve drops, carefully remove the lid.

6. With the sling, transfer the silicone tray to a wire rack. Remove the foil and paper towel. Cool for 5 minutes, uncovered. Gently loosen the edges, remove the muffins from the silicone tray, and cool on a wire rack.

TIP

If you wish, you can use a 16.9-ounce (475 g) box of premium blueberry muffin mix with canned blueberries. Each silicone baby food tray will fit half of the batter (approximately 6 ounces [170 g] of mix each). If you wish to mix up the whole box at one time, you'll still have best results if you pressure cook each tray individually. Keep the second tray of prepared muffin batter in the refrigerator while you wait for the first to cook.

HAM AND CHEESE EGG BITES

This recipe is super versatile, so change up the ingredients to match your toddler's tastes. To sneak in some vitamins with their protein, add their favorite baby food vegetable puree. This recipe is easily halved without changing the cooking time. Makes 14 bites.

Nonstick cooking spray

6 large eggs

¼ cup (60 ml) milk, half-and-half, or heavy cream

¼ teaspoon salt

⅛ teaspoon freshly ground black pepper

¼ cup (55 g) vegetable puree (broccoli, carrot, spinach), optional

½ cup (75 g) diced ham or (40 g) precooked bacon

⅓ cup (30 g) shredded cheddar cheese

1 cup (235 ml) water

1. Spray two silicone baby food trays with nonstick cooking spray. In a large bowl, whisk the eggs, milk, salt, pepper, and vegetable puree, if using, until just blended. Evenly divide the ham among the silicone cups. Pour the egg mixture over the ham until each cup is about two-thirds full. Sprinkle the cheddar cheese over each.

2. Pour 1 cup (235 ml) water into the pressure cooking pot and place a trivet in the bottom. Use a sling to carefully lower the silicone trays, stacking one on top of the other. Lock the lid in place. Select High Pressure and 9 minutes cook time for softer eggs or 11 minutes cook time for harder eggs.

3. When the cook time ends, turn off the pressure cooker. Let the pressure release naturally for 5 minutes, then finish with a quick pressure release. When the float valve drops, carefully remove the lid and use the sling to remove the trays. Place on a wire rack to cool for 5 minutes, then turn the tray over and gently squeeze to remove the egg bites from the silicone trays.

4. Serve whole or sliced, with mini-croissants or toast if desired.

TIP
You don't have to make all of the egg bites toddler-friendly! Make some for yourself by changing up the meats and cheeses or adding your own spices and mix-ins, such as:
- *Green chilies and diced tomatoes*
- *Tomatoes, mozzarella cheese, and basil*
- *Bell peppers and matchstick carrots*
- *Finely sliced fresh spinach, diced sun-dried tomatoes, and Parmesan cheese*

No matter what fillings you add, make sure you fill the cups no more than two-thirds full.

HARD-BOILED EGGS
AND AVOCADO TOAST

The pressure cooker is the best way to cook hard-boiled eggs—the shells peel easily and the eggs turn out perfect every time. Pair them with creamy avocado and cheese for a protein-packed breakfast. This recipe is easily customized to accommodate what you have on hand and can be made differently for you and your toddler. Makes 6 servings.

Hard-Boiled Eggs

6 large eggs

1 cup (235 ml) water

Avocado Toast

½ avocado

Lemon juice, to taste

Sea salt, to taste

Freshly ground black pepper, to taste

Crushed red pepper flakes, to taste, optional

6 slices good multigrain bread with seeds

Olive oil or spreadable butter

¼ cup grated cheese ([30 g] cheddar or [30 g] mozzarella) or good melting cheese (Gruyere [30 g] or Brie [36 g])

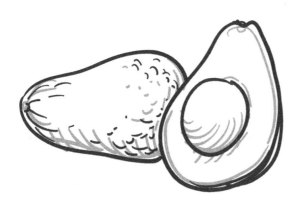

1. *Prepare the hard-boiled eggs:* Pour 1 cup (235 ml) water into the pressure cooking pot and place a steamer basket in the bottom. Carefully place the eggs on the steamer basket. Lock the lid in place. Select High Pressure and 6 minutes cook time.

2. While the eggs are cooking, fill a bowl with ice and cold water. When the cook time ends, turn off the pressure cooker. Let the pressure release naturally for 6 minutes, then finish with a quick pressure release. When the float valve drops, carefully remove the lid.

3. Immediately put the eggs into the ice water to cool. Once cool, remove eggs from water and store in the refrigerator until ready to eat, up to 1 week.

4. *Prepare the toast:* In a medium bowl, mash the avocado, lemon juice, salt, pepper, and crushed red pepper flakes, if using.

5. Serve the toast one of two ways.

   Open-faced toast: Preheat the broiler. Toast the bread to your desired doneness and then drizzle a little olive oil on each slice. Spread the mashed avocado mixture on each piece of bread. Slice the hard-boiled eggs and layer on top and then add the cheese. Place on a baking sheet, then place under the broiler to melt the cheese, 1 to 2 minutes.

Toasted sandwich: Butter each slice of bread. Turn the bread over so the buttered side is facing down. Layer the avocado, egg, and cheese on three of the slices, then top with another slice of bread, buttered side facing up. Grill in a pan on the stove over medium heat. When one side is toasted, 2 to 3 minutes, flip and toast the opposite side, 2 to 3 minutes. Slice in half to serve.

TIP

The perfect cook time for your eggs will depend on your altitude, brand of pressure cooker, and the thickness and material of your steamer basket. Some people prefer a 5-minute cook time and a 5-minute natural pressure release, while others prefer a 7-minute cook time and a 7-minute natural release. Experiment until you find your sweet spot.

If your toddler doesn't like eating big pieces of egg on their toast, you can use a cheese grater to grate the hard-boiled eggs. Combine the grated egg with the cheese and your toddler may not even notice it.

PUMPKIN-CRANBERRY-APPLE
STEEL CUT OATS

This delicious breakfast is the perfect blend of fall flavors. While the oats are a fun orange color and can stand alone, the cinnamon-pecan topping for adults and older toddlers really takes this breakfast to the next level. Makes 4 servings.

1 cup (80 g) steel cut oats

2½ cups (590 ml) water

½ cup (120 ml) heavy cream

1 cup (245 g) pumpkin puree

¼ cup (60 ml) maple syrup, plus more for serving

2 teaspoons ground cinnamon

1 teaspoon pumpkin pie spice

¼ cup (30 g) dried cranberries

¼ teaspoon salt

1 or 2 fresh apples, peeled, cored, and diced

2 tablespoons (26 g) chia seeds

Milk, for serving

Optional Cinnamon-Pecan Topping

1 cup (225 g) packed brown sugar

¼ cup (60 ml) water

1 tablespoon (7 g) ground cinnamon

⅛ teaspoon salt

2 cups (220 g) pecans, roughly chopped

1. Select Sauté and melt the butter in the pressure cooking pot. Add the oats. Toast for about 3 minutes, stirring constantly, until the oats smell nutty. Stir in the water, heavy cream, pumpkin puree, maple syrup, cinnamon, pumpkin pie spice, cranberries, and salt. Lock the lid in place. Select High Pressure and 10 minutes cook time.

2. When the cook time ends, turn off the pressure cooker. Let the pressure release naturally for 10 minutes, then finish with a quick pressure release. When the float valve drops, carefully remove the lid.

3. Stir the cooked oats in the pressure cooking pot. Add the diced apple and chia seeds and stir to combine. Replace the lid and let sit, covered, for 5 minutes.

4. *Prepare the topping:* While the oats are cooking, combine the brown sugar, water, cinnamon, and salt in a sauté pan. Bring to a boil over medium heat. (If your stove runs hot, cook over medium-low.) Add the pecans and cook, stirring constantly, until the liquid evaporates and leaves a candy coating on the pecan pieces. You can remove the pecans at any stage of this process: when all the melted sugar becomes solid and sticks to the pecans and they become "sandy" or continue stirring until the sugar melts again and gives the pecans a shiny coating. Watch closely to make sure they do not burn—especially if you're letting them get to the shiny stage.

5. Pour the pecans onto a baking sheet lined with parchment. Spread into a thin layer, separating the pecans as necessary. Let cool completely. (These can be made ahead of time, if desired.)

6. Serve topped with a splash of milk, a swirl of maple syrup, and the Cinnamon-Pecan topping, if using.

TIP

Chia seeds are an excellent thickener and an easy way to add omega-3 fatty acids to your toddler's diet. If your toddler is skeptical of the "black dots" in their food, use a coffee grinder or spice mill to grind the chia seeds prior to adding them to the oats. If you omit them, be sure to reduce the liquids added.

Some toddlers prefer crisp apple bites in their steel cut oats. However, if your child prefers more tender apples, prior to cooking the oats, place 1 cup (235 ml) water in the cooking pot and place the apples on a steamer basket. Select High Pressure and 0 minutes cook time, followed by a quick pressure release. Remove the cooked apples to a bowl, cover, and set aside. Continue the recipe as directed.

CHAPTER 2

LUNCHES

When Jennifer's boys were little, their favorite lunches were tray lunches: healthy meals with the different meats, cheeses, veggies, and fruits divided into little compartments. We've included several "three way recipes" that let you cook the protein one day and serve it three ways throughout the week. These lunch recipes are designed to minimize your cooking— serve your toddler the deconstructed meal, while you mix everything together and eat the finished dish for lunch. Be sure to reserve a toddler portion of the meat before mixing if you think your toddler will prefer the sauces and seasonings on the side.

Diced Chicken Three Ways

Shredded Chicken Three Ways

Shredded Pork Three Ways

Beef Strips Three Ways

Ground Beef Three Ways

DICED CHICKEN THREE WAYS

Chicken breasts are so versatile! Spend a few minutes cooking one day and use the chicken for meals throughout the week. These three recipes offer a variety of flavors, colors, and textures that both you and your toddler will love. Makes 3 to 4 cups (420 to 560 g) cooked chicken, to be used in the three recipes that follow.

3 large boneless, skinless chicken breasts, diced into bite-size pieces

½ teaspoon salt

½ teaspoon freshly ground black pepper

1 tablespoon (15 ml) vegetable oil

1 clove garlic, finely minced or pressed

1 cup (235 ml) reduced-sodium chicken broth

1 cup (185 g) white rice

1¼ cups (285 ml) water

1. Select Sauté to preheat the pressure cooking pot. Season the diced chicken with salt and pepper. When the pot is hot, add the vegetable oil and chicken and sauté for 3 minutes. Add the garlic and sauté for 1 minute more. Add the chicken broth and stir.

2. Place a trivet in the bottom of the pressure cooking pot. In a 7-inch (18 cm) cake pan, stir together the rice and water. Use a sling to carefully lower the pan onto the trivet. Lock the lid in place. Select High Pressure and 4 minutes cook time.

3. When the cook time ends, turn off the pressure cooker. Let the pressure release naturally for 7 minutes, then finish with a quick pressure release. When the float valve drops, carefully remove the lid. Use the sling to remove the pan from the pressure cooking pot and set the rice aside to use in the Teriyaki Bowls recipe that follows. Remove the trivet. Use an instant-read thermometer to check the chicken for doneness (see page 27).

4. Transfer the chicken to a plate to cool and discard the cooking liquid. Divide the chicken into three equal portions.

TIP
We generally like to dice the chicken into adult-size bites to ensure the chicken doesn't cook too fast (and because it's tedious to cut all of the chicken breasts that small). Once the adult portion is dished up, use kitchen shears to cut the toddler portions of chicken into appropriately sized bites.

TERIYAKI BOWLS

Makes 3 servings.

½ cup (60 g) cubed yellow squash (about ¼-inch [6 mm] cubes)

½ cup (60 g) cubed zucchini (about ¼-inch [6 mm] cubes)

¼ cup (30 g) matchstick carrots

½ cup (36 g) chopped broccoli florets

1 portion cooked cubed chicken (about 1 cup [140 g])

¼ cup (60 ml) teriyaki sauce

Cooked white rice

Chili-garlic sauce, for serving, optional

1 cup (235 ml) water

1. Add 1 cup (235 ml) water to the pressure cooking pot. Place a steamer basket in the bottom of the cooking pot and add the squash, zucchini, carrots, and broccoli. Lock the lid in place. Select High Pressure and 0 minutes cook time. When the cook time ends, turn off the pressure cooker and use a quick pressure release. When the float valve drops, carefully remove the steamer form the pot.

2. *For the toddler:* In a silicone baby food tray or small ice cube tray, fill each of the cups with a different food item—steamed veggies, cooked chicken, teriyaki sauce, rice, and diced fresh fruits.

3. *For the parent:* While the veggies steam, stir together the chicken and teriyaki sauce. To serve, top a scoop of white rice with the steamed vegetables and the teriyaki chicken mixture. Serve with chili-garlic sauce, if desired.

TIP
If your pressure cooker won't let you set the cook time for 0 minutes, select the lowest time possible, and as soon as your cooker reaches pressure, select cancel and use a quick pressure release.

STACKED GREEN ENCHILADAS

Makes 3 servings.

1 portion cooked cubed chicken (about 1 cup [140 g])

Four 4-inch (10 cm) corn or wheat tortillas

½ cup (120 g) green enchilada sauce, (128 g) green taco sauce, or (128 g) salsa verde, plus more for serving

1 cup (120 g) grated cheddar cheese

½ cup (90 g) grape tomatoes, quartered vertically

1 small can (2.25 ounces, or [63 g]) of sliced olives, optional

1 avocado, peeled, pitted, and diced, for serving

Sour cream, for serving

1 tablespoon (1 g) fresh chopped cilantro, optional

Nonstick cooking spray

1. *For the toddler:* In a silicone baby food tray or small ice cube tray, fill each of the cups with a different food item—cooked chicken, tortilla pieces, enchilada sauce, cheddar cheese, diced fresh fruits and vegetables, sour cream, and cilantro.

2. *For the parent:* Preheat the oven to 400°F (200°C, or gas mark 6). Spray a small oven-safe baking dish with nonstick cooking spray. Spoon a little enchilada sauce on the bottom of the dish. Place a tortilla on top of the enchilada sauce and sprinkle on a thin layer of cheese, followed by half of the remaining diced chicken, then the enchilada sauce, and then another thin layer of cheese. Top with another tortilla and repeat the layering process. Top with a final tortilla, the remaining enchilada sauce, and the remaining cheese. Place the dish in the oven and cook until the cheese is melted, bubbly, and just starting to brown, 5 to 10 minutes.

Remove from the oven and cool for 5 minutes. Serve topped with diced tomatoes, olives, avocado, sour cream, and cilantro.

TIP

If you like your enchiladas a little crisper, bake the tortillas in the oven until they start to brown and then sprinkle with cheese and return to the oven until melted.

CHICKEN SALAD SANDWICHES

Makes 3 servings.

1 portion cooked cubed chicken (about 1 cup [140 g])

¼ cup (38 g) quartered grapes (sliced vertically)

¼ cup (30 g) diced celery

2 tablespoons (28 g) mayonnaise

2 tablespoons (30 g) sour cream

½ teaspoon fresh lemon juice

¼ teaspoon salt

¼ teaspoon freshly ground black pepper

1 sliced green onion, white and green parts

2 tablespoons (14 g) chopped pecans, toasted, optional

3 sandwich rolls or mini croissants, halved and toasted

1. *For the toddler:* In a silicone baby food tray or small ice cube tray, fill each of the cups with a different food item—cooked chicken, sliced grapes, diced celery, cubed sandwich rolls, and diced fresh fruits and vegetables.

2. *For the parent:* In a large bowl, stir together the mayonnaise, sour cream, lemon juice, salt, and pepper. Add the cooked chicken, grapes, celery, and green onion and gently toss to combine. Cover and chill for at least 1 hour.

Just before serving, stir in the toasted pecans. Scoop the chicken salad mixture on toasted sandwich rolls or croissants.

TIP
For a lower carb option, you can serve this as a lettuce wrap.

SHREDDED CHICKEN THREE WAYS

Chicken cooked in the pressure cooker is tender, moist, and easy to shred. Here's how to cook shredded chicken in the pressure cooker and three great ways to serve it. Makes 3 to 4 cups (420 to 560 g) prepared chicken, to be used in the three recipes that follow.

3 large boneless, skinless chicken breasts

½ teaspoon salt

½ teaspoon freshly ground black pepper

1 tablespoon (15 ml) vegetable oil

1 clove garlic, finely minced or pressed

1 cup (235 ml) reduced-sodium chicken broth

1. Select Sauté to preheat the pressure cooking pot. Season the chicken with salt and pepper. When the pot is hot, add the vegetable oil and chicken and sauté for 1 to 2 minutes on each side. Add the garlic, and sauté for 1 minute more, then add the chicken broth and stir. Lock the lid in place. Select High Pressure and 4 minutes cook time.

2. When the cook time ends, turn off the pressure cooker. Use a quick pressure release. When the float valve drops, carefully remove the lid. Use an Instant-read thermometer to check the chicken for doneness (see page 27).

3. Transfer the chicken to a plate to cool and reserve the cooking liquid. Shred the chicken and divide into three equal portions.

TIP
If frozen, add the chicken and 1 cup (235 ml) water or broth. Cook under high pressure for 9 minutes, allow the pressure to release naturally for 5 minutes, then finish with a quick pressure release.

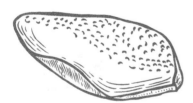

BAKED CHICKEN TAQUITOS

Makes 4 taquitos.

1 portion cooked shredded chicken (about 1 cup [140 g])

1 can (14.5 ounces) or 10 g) diced tomatoes with green chilies

¼ cup (64 g) green salsa, plus more for serving

½ teaspoon chili powder

¼ teaspoon onion powder

¼ teaspoon garlic powder

¼ teaspoon ground cumin

¼ teaspoon salt

¼ teaspoon freshly ground black pepper

2 teaspoons fresh lime juice

4 ounces (115 g) cream cheese, cubed

Four 6-inch (15 cm) flour tortillas

¾ cup (90 g) shredded Colby Jack cheese

1 tablespoon (1 g) fresh chopped cilantro leaves

1 green onion, white and green parts, chopped

Nonstick cooking spray

Guacamole and/or sour cream, for serving, optional

1. *For the toddler:* In a silicone baby food tray or small ice cube tray, fill each of the cups with a different food item—shredded chicken, tomatoes with green chilies, tortilla pieces, Colby Jack cheese, guacamole, sour cream, and diced fresh fruits and vegetables.

2. *For the parent:* Preheat the oven to 350°F (180°C, or gas mark 4). Line a baking sheet with parchment paper. In a small bowl, combine the diced tomatoes with green chilies, green salsa, chili powder, onion powder, garlic powder, cumin, salt, and pepper. Add the shredded chicken and stir until well combined. Select Sauté and cook uncovered for about 5 minutes, stirring occasionally, until all the liquid is absorbed. Stir in the lime juice. Adding a little at a time, stir in the cream cheese until melted.

Divide the chicken mixture among the tortillas. Top with the Colby Jack cheese, cilantro, and green onion. Tightly roll the tortilla around the filling. Place each taquito, seam-side down, on the prepared baking sheet. Spray the tops with cooking spray. Bake for 10 to 15 minutes until crisp and golden brown on the ends, turning seam-side up halfway through the baking time. Serve with guacamole, green salsa, and sour cream, if desired.

TIP

If you prefer a softer tortilla, you can serve this warm out of the pressure cooker. Mix in your desired amount of Colby Jack cheese when you stir in the cream cheese. Fill your tortilla with the cheesy-chicken mixture and enjoy!

ASIAN LETTUCE WRAPS

Makes 3 servings.

1 cup (235 ml) reduced-sodium chicken broth

¼ cup (63 g) hoisin sauce

2 tablespoons (28 ml) low-sodium soy sauce

¼ teaspoon chili-garlic sauce, plus more for serving

½ cup (93 g) white rice

¼ cup (31 g) canned sliced water chestnuts, drained and diced

½ cup (73 g) frozen diced carrots, thawed

1 portion cooked shredded chicken (about 1 cup [140 g])

1 cup (235 ml) water

1 green onion, white and green parts, sliced, optional

1 head butter lettuce, for serving

Sriracha, for serving, optional

1. *For the toddler:* In a silicone baby food tray or small ice cube tray, fill each of the cups with a different food item—shredded chicken, carrots, cooked rice, lettuce, and diced fresh fruits.

2. *For the Parent:* In a small round pan, stir together the chicken broth, hoisin sauce, soy sauce, and chili-garlic sauce. Stir in the rice and water chestnuts. Pour 1 cup (235 ml) water into the pressure cooking pot and place a trivet in the bottom. Use a sling to lower the pan into the pressure cooker. Lock the lid in place. Select High Pressure and 4 minutes cook time.

When the cook time ends, turn off the pressure cooker. Let the pressure release naturally for 10 minutes, then finish with a quick pressure release. When the float valve drops, carefully remove the lid.

Use the sling to remove the pan from the pressure cooking pot. Add the carrots, shredded chicken, and sliced green onion. Stir well to combine. Serve wrapped in lettuce leaves topped with more chili-garlic sauce or Sriracha, if desired.

TIP

Even though the recipe calls for a small amount, the chili-garlic sauce gives this dish a great flavor, so we prefer to add it before cooking the rice. However, if it's too spicy for your toddler, feel free to omit it and mix a little into the parent portion before serving.

QUICK CHICKEN NOODLE SOUP

Makes 3 servings.

1 tablespoon (14 g) unsalted butter

¼ cup (40 g) chopped onion

1 rib celery, chopped into ¼-inch (6 mm) pieces

2 carrots, peeled and chopped into ¼-inch (6 mm) pieces

1 clove garlic, minced

4 cups (946 ml) reduced-sodium chicken broth

1 teaspoon dried parsley

1 teaspoon salt

½ teaspoon freshly ground black pepper

1 sprig fresh thyme

1 portion cooked shredded chicken (about 1½ cups [210 g])

3 to 6 ounces (85 to 170 g) prepared egg noodles

1. Select Sauté on the pressure cooker and add the butter to the pressure cooking pot. When the butter is melted, add the onion, celery, carrots, and garlic and sauté, stirring occasionally, until tender, about 2 minutes. Add the chicken broth, dried parsley, salt, pepper, and thyme. Lock the lid in place. Select High Pressure and 0 minutes cook time.

   When the cook time ends, turn off the pressure cooker and use a quick pressure release. When the float valve drops, carefully remove the lids.

2. Remove the thyme sprig. Add the chicken and prepared egg noodles.

   TIP
   The recipe is written for vegetables cooked to crisp-tender. If you or your toddler prefers softer vegetables, increase the sauté time to 4 to 5 minutes.

SHREDDED PORK THREE WAYS

Pork shoulder cooks up tender and juicy in the pressure cooker and is a great base for lots of delicious meals. We prefer to combine the pork and seasonings for each of these meals while the pork is still hot and refrigerate the meals we're not eating so that the flavors can blend overnight. Makes 3 to 4 cups (405 to 540 g) shredded pork, to be used in the three recipes that follow.

3 pounds (1.4 kg) pork shoulder, cut into 3 large pieces

1½ teaspoons kosher salt

½ teaspoon freshly ground black pepper

1 tablespoon (15 ml) vegetable oil

1 clove garlic, finely minced or pressed

1½ cups (355 ml) water

1. Select Sauté to preheat the pressure cooking pot. Season the pork with the salt and pepper. When the pot is hot, add the vegetable oil and pork and sauté for 3 minutes on each side. Add the garlic and sauté for 1 minute more. Add the water and stir, scraping up the browned bits on the bottom of the pan. Lock the lid in place. Select High Pressure and 75 minutes cook time.

2. When the cook time ends, turn off the pressure cooker. Allow the pressure to release naturally for 10 minutes, then finish with a quick pressure release. When the float valve drops, carefully remove the lid. Use an instant-read thermometer to check the pork for doneness (see page 27).

3. Using a large fork or slotted spoon, carefully transfer the meat to a large platter and shred it with two forks. Discard any excess fat as you shred. If desired, use a fat separator to strain the juices in the cooking pot. Discard the fat and set the juices aside. Divide the pork into three equal portions.

TIP

We prefer to use pork shoulder roast in the pressure cooker because pork sirloin roast are leaner and don't cook up as tender.

QUICK CARNITAS STREET TACOS

Makes 3 servings.

1 portion cooked shredded pork (about 1 cup [135 g])

¼ cup (60 ml) reserved cooking liquid

¼ teaspoon dried oregano

⅛ teaspoon ground cumin

½ teaspoon onion powder

½ teaspoon garlic powder

Salt and freshly ground black pepper

2 tablespoons (28 ml) fresh orange juice

Small 4-inch (10 cm) corn tortillas, guacamole, queso fresco, fresh chopped cilantro, lime juice, and sour cream, for serving

1. *For the toddler:* In a silicone baby food tray or small ice cube tray, fill each of the cups with a different food item—shredded pork, corn tortilla pieces, guacamole, queso fresco, sour cream, and diced fresh fruits and vegetables.

2. *For the parent:* Preheat the broiler. In a small bowl, combine the reserved cooking liquid, oregano, cumin, onion powder, garlic powder, salt, pepper, and orange juice. Add the pork and stir until well combined.

   Line a rimmed baking sheet with aluminum foil and spread the shredded pork in a single layer. Broil for 3 to 5 minutes or until the edges of the pork start to brown and crisp.

Serve in warmed tortillas topped with guacamole, queso fresco, cilantro, a squeeze of lime juice, and sour cream, as desired.

TIP

As your child grows, you'll want to slowly start to introduce the spices you enjoy into their food as well.

KALUA PORK

Makes 3 servings.

1 portion cooked shredded pork (about 1 cup [135 g])

½ cup (120 ml) reserved cooking liquid

1 to 2 teaspoons kosher salt, to taste

1 to 2 teaspoons liquid smoke, to taste

Cooked rice, steamed broccoli, carrot sticks, and fresh fruit (pineapple, mangoes), for serving

1. *For the toddler:* In a silicone baby food tray or small ice cube tray, fill each of the cups with a different food item—shredded pork, rice, broccoli, carrots, and diced fresh fruit.

2. *For the parent:* In a small bowl, combine the reserved cooking liquid, salt, and liquid smoke. Add the pork and stir until well combined.

Serve over cooked rice with a side of steamed broccoli, carrot sticks, and fresh fruit, as desired.

TIP
Start with less salt and liquid smoke and then add more as desired.

PULLED PORK SANDWICHES

Makes 3 or 4 sandwiches.

1 portion cooked shredded pork (about 1 cup [135 g])

¼ cup (60 ml) reserved cooking liquid

¼ cup (65 g) barbecue sauce, plus more for serving

3 or 4 sandwich rolls, toasted

1. *For the toddler:* In a silicone baby food tray or small ice cube tray, fill each of the cups with a different food item—shredded pork, barbecue sauce, cubed sandwich rolls, and diced fresh fruits and vegetables.

2. *For the parent:* In a small bowl, combine the reserved cooking liquid and barbecue sauce. Add the shredded pork and stir to combine. Serve on toasted rolls with more barbecue sauce, if desired.

TIP
You can mix the pork and reheat it in the microwave at 50 percent power for 1 minute at a time until it reaches the desired temperature.

BEEF STRIPS THREE WAYS

Sirloin steak is a lean cut of beef that is quick cooking and versatile, and cooking it in the pressure cooker helps tenderize the meat. Makes about 4 cups (600 g) beef strips, to be used in the three recipes that follow.

2 pounds (900 g) boneless beef sirloin steak, cut against the grain into ¼-inch (6 mm)-thick slices

Salt and freshly ground black pepper

1 tablespoon (15 ml) vegetable oil, plus more as needed

½ cup (120 ml) reduced-sodium beef broth

½ teaspoon garlic powder

1. Select Sauté to preheat the pressure cooking pot. Season the beef strips with salt and pepper. Add the vegetable oil to the pressure cooking pot and quickly brown the beef strips on one side. Work in batches until all the meat is browned on one side. Add more oil if needed. Transfer the meat to a plate when browned.

2. Add the beef broth, garlic powder, ½ teaspoon salt, and ½ teaspoon pepper to the cooking pot and stir, scraping up the browned bits on the bottom of the pan. Return the browned beef to the pot.

3. Lock the lid in place. Select High Pressure and 12 minutes cook time. When the cook time ends, turn off the pressure cooker. Use a quick pressure release. When the float valve drops, carefully remove the lid. Use an instant-read thermometer to check the beef for doneness (see page 27).

4. Transfer the beef to a plate to cool and reserve the cooking liquid. Divide the beef into three equal portions.

TIP
The browning process makes a big difference in the flavor of the cooked beef, so if at all possible, don't skip this step.

ASIAN BEEF BOWLS

Makes 3 servings.

1 portion cooked beef strips (about 1½ cups [225 g])

¼ cup (60 ml) reduced-sodium beef broth

¼ cup (60 ml) low-sodium soy sauce

1 tablespoon (15 g) packed light brown sugar

¼ teaspoon onion powder

¼ teaspoon garlic powder

2 teaspoons sesame oil

Dash of red pepper flakes

1 tablespoon (8 g) cornstarch

1 tablespoon (15 ml) cold water

1 cup (71 g) chopped broccoli, lightly steamed

Cooked rice and toasted sesame seeds, for serving

1. *For the toddler:* In a silicone baby food tray or small ice cube tray, fill each of the cups with a different food item—beef strips, steamed broccoli, soy sauce, and diced fresh fruit.

2. *For the parent:* In the pressure cooking pot, combine the beef broth, soy sauce, brown sugar, onion powder, garlic powder, sesame oil, and red pepper flakes, stirring until the sugar dissolves.

   In a small bowl, whisk the cornstarch and 1 tablespoon (15 ml) cold water until smooth. Select Sauté and add the slurry to the pot, whisking constantly until the sauce comes to a boil and thickens. Stir in the beef strips and steamed broccoli.

Serve over cooked rice and garnish with toasted sesame seeds, if desired.

TIP
You can cook the sauce on the stovetop, if desired.

SMOTHERED BEEF BURRITOS

Makes 3 servings.

1 portion cooked beef strips (about 1½ cups [225 g])

¼ cup (60 ml) reduced-sodium beef broth

1 tablespoon (8 g) chili powder

¼ teaspoon smoked paprika

¼ teaspoon ground cumin

¼ teaspoon garlic powder

¼ teaspoon dried oregano

Salt and freshly ground pepper

3 burrito-size flour tortillas

Shredded cheese, Mexican rice, and black beans, for filling, optional

Enchilada sauce, sour cream, guacamole, and fresh salsa, for serving, optional

1. *For the toddler:* In a silicone baby food tray or small ice cube tray, fill each of the cups with a different food item—beef strips, shredded cheese, Mexican rice, black beans, enchilada sauce, sour cream, guacamole, and diced fresh fruits and vegetables.

2. *For the parent:* Preheat the broiler. In the pressure cooking pot, combine the beef broth, chili powder, paprika, cumin, garlic powder, oregano, and salt and pepper to taste. Add the beef strips, select Sauté, and stir until the spices are incorporated and the beef is warmed through.

Use a slotted spoon to place ½ cup (75 g) warmed beef in the center of a tortilla and add shredded cheese and additional fillings of your choice. Fold in the edges and roll up tightly into a burrito. Repeat with the remaining tortillas. Top the burritos with your favorite enchilada sauce and more shredded cheese. Place on a baking sheet lined with parchment and broil for 2 to 4 minutes until the cheese is bubbly. (Watch closely because the cheese browns quickly once it starts.) Serve topped with sour cream, guacamole, and fresh salsa, if desired.

TIP
Reheat the beef strips after mixing with the broth to keep the meat from drying out.

BEEF AND CHEDDAR SANDWICHES

Makes 3 sandwiches.

1 tablespoon (14 g) unsalted butter

1 tablespoon (8 g) all-purpose flour

½ cup (120 ml) milk

Pinch of cayenne pepper, optional

Pinch of salt

¾ cup (90 g) shredded cheddar cheese

3 rolls or hamburger buns, toasted

1 portion cooked beef strips
(about 1½ cups [225 g])

1. *For the toddler:* In a silicone baby food tray or small ice cube tray, fill each of the cups with a different food item—cheese sauce (recipe follows), diced buns, shredded beef, and diced fresh fruits and vegetables.

2. *For the parent:* In a small saucepan over medium heat, melt the butter. Sprinkle in the flour and cook until bubbling, stirring constantly. Gradually whisk in the milk, a little at a time, until the sauce is smooth and thick. Whisk in the cayenne and salt. Add the cheddar cheese a handful at a time and stir until melted and smooth. Remove from the heat.

To serve, top each bun with warmed beef strips and ladle the cheese sauce on top.

TIP
If you'd prefer, replace the cayenne pepper with ½ to 1 teaspoon hot sauce (we used Frank's RedHot). It doesn't add much heat, but it does add a great flavor to the cheese sauce.

GROUND BEEF THREE WAYS

Ground beef is a staple in most families. It's relatively inexpensive and easy to find a flavor that everyone loves. Makes about 3 cups (675 g) ground beef, to be used in the three recipes that follow.

2 pounds (900 g) ground beef

½ teaspoon salt

½ teaspoon freshly ground black pepper

1 tablespoon (15 ml) vegetable oil

1 clove garlic, finely minced or pressed

1½ cups (355 ml) reduced-sodium beef broth

1. Select Sauté to preheat the pressure cooking pot. Season the ground beef with the salt and pepper. When the pot is hot, add the vegetable oil and ground beef and sauté for 3 minutes. Add the garlic, sauté for 1 minute more, and then add the beef broth and stir. Lock the lid in place. Select High Pressure and 3 minutes cook time.

2. When the cook time ends, turn off the pressure cooker. Use a quick pressure release. When the float valve drops, carefully remove the lid. Use an instant-read thermometer to check the cooked ground beef for doneness (see page 27).

3. Transfer the ground beef to a plate to cool and discard the cooking liquid. Divide the ground beef into three equal portions.

TIP

Use a chopper spatula to help break up the ground beef while sautéing.

GROUND BEEF TACOS

Makes 3 servings.

1 portion cooked ground beef (about 1 cup [225 g])

2 teaspoons chili powder

½ teaspoon ground cumin

½ teaspoon garlic powder

1 teaspoon onion powder

¼ teaspoon salt

Dash of cayenne pepper

Hard (or soft) taco shells, lettuce, salsa, shredded cheese, diced tomatoes, and sour cream, for serving

1. *For the toddler:* In a silicone baby food tray or small ice cube tray, fill each of the cups with a different food item—cooked ground beef, shredded cheese, diced tomatoes, sour cream, and diced fresh fruits and vegetables.

2. *For the parent:* In a bowl, mix the beef, chili powder, cumin, garlic powder, onion powder, salt and cayenne pepper. Serve in hard taco shells with lettuce, salsa, shredded cheese, diced tomatoes, and sour cream.

TIP

If you'd prefer, you can substitute a tablespoon (8 g) of your favorite taco seasoning mix for the spices listed here.

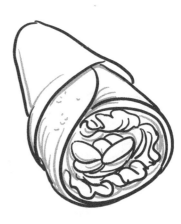

LOADED BAKED POTATOES

Makes 3 servings.

3 russet potatoes

2 tablespoons (28 g) unsalted butter

1 portion cooked ground beef (about 1 cup [225 g])

½ cup (36 g) steamed chopped broccoli

¼ cup (30 g) grated cheddar cheese

3 slices bacon, cooked and crumbled, optional

¼ cup (60 ml) ranch dressing or (60 g) sour cream

1 teaspoon minced chives or thinly sliced green onions

1 cup (235 ml) water

1. Add 1 cup (235 ml) water to the pressure cooking pot and place a trivet in the bottom. Place the potatoes on the trivet. Lock the lid in place. Select High Pressure and 25 minutes cook time.

   When the cook time ends, turn off the pressure cooker. Let the pressure release naturally for 5 minutes, then finish with a quick pressure release. When the float valve drops, carefully remove the lid. Use an instant-read thermometer to check that the potatoes reach 205°F (96°C) in the center. If needed, re-cover the pot and let them steam for a few minutes longer.

2. *For the toddler:* In a silicone baby food tray or small ice cube tray, fill each of the cups with a different food item—cooked ground beef, diced potato, broccoli, cheese, bacon, ranch dressing, and diced fresh fruits and vegetables.

3. *For the parent:* Slice the potatoes lengthwise and load them with butter, ground beef, broccoli, shredded cheese, and crumbled bacon. Drizzle with the ranch dressing and sprinkle with chives.

TIP
You can make this twice-baked or mashed-potato style; just scoop the potato out of the skins (leaving a little extra if you're doing twice-baked) and then combine with milk, butter, and cheese. Mash together with a fork until well mixed. Spoon back into the potato skins, top with more cheese, and serve.

PASTA RAGU

Makes 3 servings.

1 portion cooked ground beef (about 1 cup [225 g])

1½ cups (375 g) marinara sauce, store-bought or homemade (page 95)

1 tablespoon (3 g) chopped fresh basil, optional

2½ cups (570 ml) water, plus more as needed

1 teaspoon salt

1 tablespoon (15 ml) vegetable oil

8 ounces (225 g) rotini pasta

Freshly grated Parmesan cheese, for serving

1. *For the toddler:* In a silicone baby food tray or small ice cube tray, fill each of the cups with a different food item—cooked ground beef, marinara sauce, pasta, Parmesan cheese, and diced fresh fruits and vegetables.

2. *For the parent:* In a bowl, stir together the ground beef, marinara sauce, and fresh basil. Set aside.

   Add the water, salt, vegetable oil, and pasta to the pressure cooking pot. If needed, add more water to just cover the pasta—do not stir. Lock the lid in place. Select High Pressure and 4 minutes cook time.

When the cook time ends, turn off the pressure cooker. Use a quick pressure release, or, if necessary, an intermittent pressure release. When the float valve drops, carefully remove the lid. Ladle off any excess water from the pasta.

Serve the pasta topped with marinara sauce and freshly grated Parmesan cheese.

TIP

If you wish to substitute a different noodle, set your pressure cooker to cook at High Pressure for half the cook time on the package minus 1 minute.

CHAPTER 3

DINNERS

We have chosen not to cook separate meals for toddlers—we want them to start eating the foods and flavors the whole family enjoys. These dinner recipes are easily customized to be toddler-friendly while still representing a meal that parents are happy to eat.

CRISPY CHICKEN FINGERS

These fresh chicken strips are breaded and baked—not fried—so they're a better-for-you meal you can feel good about enjoying with your toddler. Makes 4 servings.

1½ cups (168 g) panko (Japanese-style bread crumbs)

1 tablespoon (15 ml) olive oil

10 to 12 chicken tenders (1 to 1½ pounds [455 to 680 g])

2 to 3 teaspoons (12-18 g) salt, divided

1 teaspoon freshly ground black pepper, divided

½ cup (120 ml) chicken broth

½ cup (50 g) freshly grated Parmesan cheese

½ cup (63 g) all-purpose flour

½ teaspoon garlic powder

3 or 4 large egg whites

2 tablespoons (28 ml) water

Nonstick cooking spray

Ketchup or ranch dressing, for serving, optional

1. In a 12-inch (30 cm) skillet, stir together the panko and olive oil. Toast the panko over medium heat, stirring often, until golden, about 8 minutes. (Watch closely because the panko can burn quickly.) When toasted, spread the panko in a shallow dish to cool.

2. In the pressure cooking pot, combine the chicken tenders, 1 teaspoon of salt, ½ teaspoon of pepper, and chicken broth. Lock the lid in place. Select High Pressure and 2 minutes cook time.

3. When the cook time ends, turn off the pressure cooker. Allow the pressure to release naturally for 3 minutes and then finish with a quick pressure release. When the float valve drops, carefully remove the lid. Transfer the chicken to a paper towel–lined plate.

4. Adjust the oven rack to the middle position and preheat the oven to 475°F (240°C or gas mark 9). In a first shallow dish, stir together the cooled panko and the grated Parmesan cheese. In a second shallow dish, add the flour, garlic powder, remaining 1 to 2 teaspoons salt, and remaining ½ teaspoon pepper, and stir until well combined. In a third shallow dish, whisk together the egg whites and 2 tablespoons (28 ml) water.

5. Line a rimmed baking sheet with foil, place a wire rack on top, and spray the rack with a generous amount of nonstick cooking spray.

6. Lightly dredge each chicken tender in the egg whites, shaking off the excess. Dip in the flour mixture, shaking off the excess. Dip into the egg whites again, shaking off the excess. Finally, coat each chicken tender in the toasted panko, pressing the bread crumbs into the chicken strips to make sure they adhere. Lay the chicken on the wire rack.

7. Spray the tops of the chicken with nonstick cooking spray. Bake for 3 minutes, then flip and bake for 3 minutes more. Use an instant-read thermometer to check the chicken for doneness (see page 27).

8. Serve with fresh fruits and vegetables, along with ketchup, ranch dressing, or another sauce for dipping.

Chicken Parmesan Variation

Add an extra teaspoon of garlic powder to the flour mixture. Prepare as directed. Bake at 475°F (240°C or gas mark 9) for 3 minutes. Remove the chicken from the oven. Flip each piece of chicken and add marinara sauce, store-bought or homemade (page 95), and grated mozzarella cheese. Bake for 5 minutes longer or until the cheese is melted. Serve over cooked pasta, topped with sauce and additional mozzarella and Parmesan cheese.

TIP

These breaded chicken strips freeze very well! If you want, you can cook up a double or triple batch. (You may need to add another minute to the cook time.) After baking, allow to cool to room temperature. In a freezer-safe zipper-top plastic bag, lay the chicken strips flat, separated by parchment paper. When ready to cook, take directly from the freezer to a preheated oven and cook at 400°F (200°C or gas mark 6) for 5 to 10 minutes, checking periodically.

CHEESY POTATOES

Always a hit at any meal, these ooey-gooey cheesy potatoes have a crisp buttery topping that you and your toddler will love. Makes 4 servings.

5 tablespoons (70 g) unsalted butter, divided

¼ cup (40 g) chopped onion

1 cup (235 ml) reduced-sodium chicken broth

1 teaspoon salt

¼ teaspoon freshly ground black pepper

1 bag (20 ounces, or 560 g) shredded fresh hashbrown potatoes

Nonstick cooking spray

1 cup (112 g) panko bread crumbs

⅓ cup (77 g) sour cream

1 cup (115 g) shredded Monterey Jack cheese

1. Select Sauté and melt 2 tablespoons (28 g) of the butter in the pressure cooking pot. Add the onion. Sauté for about 3 minutes, stirring occasionally, until tender. Add the chicken broth, salt, and pepper. Put the steamer basket in the cooking pot and add the potatoes. Lock the lid in place. Select High Pressure and 3 minutes cook time.

2. While the potatoes cook, preheat the broiler. Spray a 9 x 13-inch (23 x 33 cm) ovenproof dish with nonstick cooking spray. In a small microwave-safe bowl, melt the remaining 3 tablespoons (42 g) butter and stir in the panko. Set aside.

3. When the cook time ends, turn off the pressure cooker and use a quick pressure release. When the float valve drops, carefully remove the lid. Remove the steamer basket with the potatoes and transfer the potatoes to the prepared dish.

4. Stir the sour cream and Monterey Jack cheese into the cooking liquid in the pot and pour the mixture over the potatoes. Use two forks to gently mix the sauce with the potatoes. Top with the panko topping and broil for 5 to 7 minutes or until golden brown.

TIP

If you like, substitute the shredded potatoes with five potatoes, thinly sliced, and increase the cook time by 2 minutes.

BROCCOLI CHEESY CHICKEN AND RICE

Layered pot-in-pot cooking in the pressure cooker allows you to cook your whole dinner at the same time. In this dish, the rice cooks in a separate pot right on top of the chicken. Makes 4 servings.

1 large boneless, skinless chicken breast, cut into bite-size pieces

Salt and freshly ground black pepper

1 tablespoon (15 ml) olive oil

¼ cup (40 g) chopped onion

1 tablespoon (14 g) unsalted butter

1 cup (235 ml) reduced-sodium chicken broth

¼ teaspoon salt

¼ teaspoon pepper

2 teaspoons dried parsley

1 cup (185 g) white rice

1¼ cups (285 ml) water

2 tablespoons (16 g) cornstarch

2 tablespoons (28 ml) cold water

2 ounces (55 g) cream cheese, cut into cubes

½ cup (58 g) shredded cheddar cheese, plus more for garnishing

1 cup (71 g) chopped broccoli, lightly steamed, for serving

Red pepper flakes, optional

1. Season the chicken with salt and pepper to taste. Select Sauté to preheat the pressure cooking pot. When hot, add the olive oil and the onion and sauté for 1 minute. Add the diced chicken and butter and sauté for 2 minutes more. Stir in the chicken broth, ¼ teaspoon salt, ¼ teaspoon pepper, and the parsley.

2. Place a trivet in the bottom of the pressure cooking pot over the chicken. In a 7-inch (18 cm) cake pan, stir together the rice and 1¼ cups (285 ml) water. Use a sling to carefully lower the pan onto the rack. Lock the lid in place. Select High Pressure and 4 minutes cook time.

3. When the cook time ends, turn off the pressure cooker. Allow the pressure to release naturally for 10 minutes and then use a quick pressure release. When the float valve drops, carefully remove the lid. Use an instant-read thermometer to check the chicken for doneness (see page 27).

4. Use the sling to remove the pan from the cooking pot. Remove the trivet. (If your toddler doesn't like sauce on their meat, use a slotted spoon to remove their chicken to a bowl and set aside.)

5. In a small bowl, whisk the cornstarch and 2 tablespoons (28 ml) cold water until smooth. Select Sauté and add the slurry to the pot, stirring constantly. Add the cream cheese and cheddar cheese, stirring until melted.

6. Serve the cheesy chicken over the rice and steamed broccoli and garnish with more cheddar cheese, if desired. Season with additional salt, black pepper, or red pepper flakes to taste.

TIP

You can steam the broccoli in the pressure cooker if you prefer. After pressure cooking, remove the rice from the cake pan to a serving bowl. Place the broccoli in the cake pan and return the pan to the cooking pot. Replace the lid and allow the broccoli to steam in the cooking pot until fork tender, 2 to 4 minutes. Use a quick pressure release. When the float valve drops, carefully remove the lid. Remove the cake pan and trivet and continue with the recipe as directed.

FIESTA CHICKEN SALAD

If salads are a little too adventurous for your toddler, you can serve the chicken and rice mixture in a taco shell, using the homemade salad dressing as a dip. Makes 4 servings.

Cilantro-Lime Dressing

3 tablespoons (32 g) Hidden Valley Ranch Dressing Mix

1 cup (225 g) mayonnaise

½ cup (120 ml) milk or buttermilk

1 tablespoon (15 ml) fresh lime juice

2 cloves garlic, minced or pressed

½ cup (8 g) chopped fresh cilantro

¼ cup (64 g) mild green salsa

¼ teaspoon red pepper flakes, optional

Cilantro-Lime Chicken and Rice

1 tablespoon (15 ml) extra virgin olive oil

1 pound (455 g) ground chicken

2 tablespoons (20 g) finely chopped onion

1 cup (235 ml) reduced-sodium chicken broth

½ cup (93 g) long-grain white rice

1 teaspoon salt

½ teaspoon ground cumin

¼ teaspoon black pepper

1 can (10 ounces, or 280 g) of diced tomatoes with green chilies (Rotel Mild)

1 tablespoon (15 ml) fresh lime juice

1 tablespoon (8 g) cornstarch

1 tablespoon (15 ml) cold water

¼ cup (4 g) chopped fresh cilantro

1 can (14.5 ounces, or 410 g) of black beans, drained and rinsed

2 cups (94 g) shredded romaine

1 cup (180 g) chopped tomatoes, for serving, optional

1 avocado, peeled, pitted, and diced, for serving, optional

Shredded cheddar cheese, for serving

1. *Prepare the dressing:* In a blender jar, combine ranch dressing mix, mayonnaise, milk, lime juice, garlic, cilantro, green salsa, and red pepper flakes, if using. Pulse until well combined. Refrigerate for several hours or overnight.

2. *Prepare the chicken and rice:* Select Sauté to preheat the pressure cooking pot. When the pot is hot, add the olive oil and chicken. Cook for about 5 minutes, crumbling with a spoon, until browned. Add the onion and cook for 1 minute more, stirring frequently. Stir in the chicken broth, rice, salt, cumin, black pepper, diced tomatoes with green chilies, and lime juice. Lock the lid in place. Select High Pressure and 4 minutes cook time.

3. When the cook time ends, turn off the pressure cooker. Let the pressure release naturally for 10 minutes and then finish with a quick pressure release. When the float valve drops, carefully remove the lid.

4. In a small bowl, whisk the cornstarch and cold water until smooth. Add the slurry to the pot. Select Sauté and cook, stirring constantly, until the sauce reaches your desired thickness. Stir in the cilantro and black beans.

5. Serve over the shredded lettuce, with tomatoes, avocado, and cheese and a drizzle of Cilantro-Lime Dressing on top.

TIP

The Cilantro-Lime Dressing keeps in the refrigerator for up to 2 weeks, and we love to drizzle a little over tacos or vegetables or even use it as a chip dip.

CREAMY CASHEW CHICKEN AND BROCCOLI

Based on an award-wining recipe, the whole family will love this cashew chicken cooked with a hint of rosemary and drizzled in rich Gouda cheese. Makes 4 servings.

Cashew Chicken

1 tablespoon (15 ml) olive oil

¼ cup (40 g) finely diced red onion

1 tablespoon (14 g) unsalted butter

2 large boneless, skinless chicken breasts (about 1 pound [455 g]), diced into bite-size pieces

½ cup (120 ml) reduced-sodium chicken broth

½ teaspoon crushed rosemary leaves

1 cup (185 g) white rice

1¼ cups (285 ml) water

2 tablespoons (16 g) cornstarch

2 tablespoons (28 ml) cold water

½ cup (70 g) cashews, coarsely chopped

1 cup (71 g) chopped broccoli, lightly steamed, for serving

Gouda Cream Sauce

2 tablespoons (28 g) unsalted butter

2 tablespoons (16 g) all-purpose flour

1 cup (235 ml) half-and-half, plus more if needed

5 slices of Gouda cheese

Salt and freshly ground black pepper

1. *Prepare the Cashew Chicken:* Select Sauté to preheat the pressure cooking pot. When the pot is hot, add the olive oil and onion to the cooking pot and sauté for 1 minute. Add 1 tablespoon (28 g) butter and the diced chicken and sauté for 2 minutes more. Add the chicken broth and rosemary.

2. Place a trivet in the bottom of the pressure cooking pot over the chicken. In a 7-inch (18 cm) cake pan, stir together the rice and 1¼ cups (285 ml) water. Use a sling to carefully lower the pan onto the rack. Lock the lid in place. Select High Pressure and 4 minutes cook time.

3. *Prepare the Gouda cream sauce:* While the chicken and rice are cooking, in a small saucepan on the stovetop over medium heat, melt the 2 tablespoons (28 g) butter. Whisk in the flour. Cook for 2 to 3 minutes, stirring constantly, until smooth and bubbly. Gradually add the half-and-half, stirring constantly, until the sauce is thick and smooth, about 2 minutes. Reduce the heat to low and add the Gouda cheese, a little at a time, until smooth and creamy. Add more half-and-half, if necessary, to thin the sauce to

the desired consistency. Season with salt and pepper to taste. Remove from the heat. (If your pressure cooker can sauté on a low heat setting, you can choose to do this step in your pressure cooker.)

4. When the cook time ends, turn off the pressure cooker. Allow the pressure to release naturally for 10 minutes, then use a quick pressure release. When the float valve drops, carefully remove the lid. Use the sling to remove the cake pan and set aside. Remove the trivet.

5. In a small bowl, mix the cornstarch and 2 tablespoons (28 ml) cold water until smooth. Select Sauté and add the slurry to the pot and cook, stirring constantly, until the liquid thickens. Stir in ½ cup (120 ml) of the Gouda Cream Sauce and the cashews.

6. Serve the chicken over the rice and steamed broccoli, topped with extra Gouda Cream Sauce.

TIP
If you don't have red onions on hand, you can substitute white or yellow onions.

BUTTERY SPICED CHICKEN AND NOODLES

This is another great one-pot meal! The spaghetti cooks on the bottom while the chicken cooks on the top—coated in spices and browned in butter. After cooking, the chicken is made into in a rich, colorful cream sauce to serve on top of the pasta. Makes 4 servings.

Nonstick cooking spray

1 teaspoon garlic powder

½ teaspoon onion powder

½ teaspoon chili powder

½ teaspoon paprika

½ teaspoon salt

¼ teaspoon black pepper

1 pound (455 g) chicken tenders (about 6 strips)

1 tablespoon (14 g) unsalted butter

1 tablespoon (15 ml) vegetable oil

¼ cup (60 ml) reduced-sodium chicken broth

6 ounces (170 g) spaghetti, broken in half

2 cups (475 ml) water

1 tablespoon (8 g) cornstarch

1 tablespoon (15 ml) cold water

1 cup (235 ml) heavy cream

1 tablespoon (1 g) dried parsley

1. Coat a 7-inch (18 cm) cake pan with nonstick cooking spray. Set aside.

2. In a mixing bowl, combine the garlic powder, onion powder, chili powder, paprika, salt, and pepper. Add the chicken and toss to coat the chicken with the spices.

3. Select Sauté and preheat the pressure cooking pot. When the pot is hot, add the butter and vegetable oil and stir until the butter is melted. Add the chicken and sauté on both sides, about 2 minutes per side. Remove the chicken to the prepared cake pan. Pour the chicken broth into the cooking pot to deglaze the pan. Scrape the browned bits off of the bottom of the pan and pour over the chicken in the cake pan. Wipe out the cooking pot with a paper towel.

4. Place the spaghetti in the pressure cooking pot. Pour in enough water to just cover the spaghetti noodles, about 2 cups (475 ml). Place a tall trivet in the cooking pot over the spaghetti and use a sling to carefully lower the cake pan on top. Lock the lid in place. Select High Pressure and 4 minutes cook time.

5. When the cook time ends, turn off the pressure cooker. Allow the pressure to release naturally for 2 minutes, then use a quick pressure release. When the float valve drops, carefully remove the lid. Use an instant-read thermometer to check the chicken for doneness (see page 27).

6. Use the sling to carefully remove the cake pan from the cooking pot. Remove the trivet. Pour the spaghetti into a strainer to drain. Return the contents of the cake pan to the pressure cooking pot. (If your toddler doesn't like sauce on their chicken, use a slotted spoon to remove their portion to a bowl and set aside.)

7. In a small bowl, dissolve the cornstarch in the 1 tablespoon (15 ml) cold water. Push the chicken to one side of the cooking pot and add the cornstarch slurry. Select Sauté and cook, stirring constantly, until the sauce thickens. Turn off the pressure cooker and stir in the heavy cream and parsley.

8. Serve the chicken and sauce over the spaghetti noodles along with your toddler's favorite vegetables.

TIP

When you're in a hurry, you can place the chicken and spices in a zipper-top plastic bag and shake to evenly coat the chicken.

DECONSTRUCTED CHICKEN POT PIE

This toddler spin on classic chicken pot pie features a thicker, easier-to-eat sauce and fun pie dough cutouts that your toddler can pick up and eat with their fingers. Makes 4 servings.

1 piecrust, store-bought or homemade (recipe follows)

1 tablespoon (15 ml) vegetable oil

½ cup (80 g) diced onion

1 rib celery, chopped

½ cup (120 ml) reduced-sodium chicken broth

2 large boneless, skinless chicken breasts (about 1 pound [455 g]), diced into bite-size pieces

1 large russet potato, cut into 1-inch (2.5 cm) cubes

½ teaspoon salt

¼ teaspoon freshly ground black pepper

1 cup (140 g) frozen carrots and peas, steamed

⅓ cup (75 g) unsalted butter

⅓ cup (42 g) all-purpose flour

½ cup (120 ml) milk, plus more as needed

1. Preheat the oven to 425°F (220°C, or gas mark 7). Line a baking sheet with parchment paper (or spray with nonstick cooking spray) and set aside. Roll out the piecrust dough to ⅛ inch (3 mm) thick. Use cookie cutters to create shapes in the piecrust and transfer to the baking sheet. Bake according to the package directions until lightly browned. Remove from the oven and allow to cool.

2. Select Sauté to preheat the pressure cooking pot. When hot, add the vegetable oil, onion, and celery. Sauté for about 3 minutes, stirring occasionally, until the onion is tender. Stir in the chicken broth, diced chicken, potato, salt, and pepper. Lock the lid in place. Select High Pressure and 4 minutes cook time.

3. When the cook time ends, turn off the pressure cooker. Use a quick pressure release. When the float valve drops, carefully remove the lid. Use an instant-read thermometer to check the chicken for doneness (see page 27).

4. Stir in the carrots and peas.

5. In a small saucepan on the stovetop over medium heat, melt the butter. Whisk in the flour. Cook for 2 to 3 minutes, stirring constantly, until smooth and bubbly. Gradually add the milk, stirring constantly for about 2 minutes, until the sauce is thick and smooth. Add this to the pressure cooking pot and stir until the sauce is thick and creamy. Add more milk, if needed, to achieve your desired consistency.

6. To serve, place the cooked pot pie filling into individual bowls and top with the baked piecrust shapes.

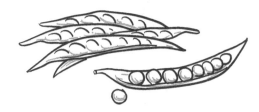

HOMEMADE PIECRUST

1¼ cups (156 g) all-purpose flour, plus more for rolling the dough

½ teaspoon salt

2 tablespoons (28 g) unsalted butter, chilled

⅓ cup (75 g) shortening, chilled (we prefer butter-flavored shortening)

3 tablespoons (45 ml) ice water

1. In a large bowl, combine the flour and salt. Cut the butter and shortening into small cubes and add them to the flour mixture. Use a pastry cutter or two knives to cut the butter and shortening into the flour until it resembles very coarse meal.

2. One tablespoon (15 ml) at a time, add the ice water to the dough, mixing it in with a fork. Add just enough water so the dough holds together when you squeeze a handful. (It will still look dry and crumbly.) Form the dough into a round disk and wrap it in plastic wrap. Chill for 30 minutes.

3. On a well-floured surface, roll the dough into a 12-inch (30 cm) circle that's ⅛ inch (3 mm) thick. Use the cookie cutters to cut out fun shapes and then bake at 425°F (220°C, or gas mark 7) for 15 to 20 minutes until lightly browned.

TIP
Most toddlers love using the cookie cutters to help cut out the piecrust pieces. However, because toddlers don't have the best sense of where to position the cookie cutter, you can let them have their turn first and then use a knife to cut the leftover crust into shapes and bake it all

SWEET ASIAN CHICKEN AND RICE

Kids love this mild, sweet honey sauce, so this meal is likely to become part of your regular rotation. The sesame oil is the secret ingredient that makes this dish; even though it's just a small amount, don't skip it! Makes 4 servings.

2 large boneless, skinless chicken breasts (about 1 pound [455 g]), diced

Salt and freshly ground black pepper

1 tablespoon (15 ml) vegetable oil

¼ cup (40 g) diced onion

1 clove of garlic, minced

¼ cup (60 ml) low-sodium soy sauce

¼ cup (31 g) chopped water chestnuts

1 tablespoon (16 g) tomato paste

⅛ teaspoon red pepper flakes

1 cup (185 g) white rice

1¼ cups (285 ml) water

1 teaspoon sesame oil

¼ cup (85 g) honey

1 tablespoon (8 g) cornstarch

1 tablespoon (15 ml) cold water

1 green onion, white and green parts, chopped

1. Season the chicken with salt and pepper. Select Sauté to preheat the pressure cooking pot. When the pot is hot, add the vegetable oil, onion, garlic, and chicken. Sauté for about 3 minutes, stirring occasionally, until the onion softens. Stir in the soy sauce, water chestnuts, tomato paste, and red pepper flakes.

2. Place a trivet in the bottom of the pressure cooking pot over the chicken. In a 7-inch (18 cm) cake pan, stir together the rice and water. Use a sling to carefully lower the pan onto the rack. Lock the lid in place. Select High Pressure and 4 minutes cook time.

3. When the cook time ends, turn off the pressure cooker. Allow the pressure to release naturally for 7 minutes, then use a quick pressure release. When the valve drops, carefully remove the lid. Use the sling to remove the pan from the cooking pot. Remove the trivet. Use an instant-read thermometer to check the chicken for doneness (see page 27).

4. Add the sesame oil and honey to the pot and stir to combine.

5. In a small bowl, whisk the cornstarch and 1 tablespoon (15 ml) cold water until smooth. Add the slurry to the pot. Select Sauté and simmer, stirring constantly, until the sauce thickens. Stir in the green onions. Serve over the rice.

TIP
If you want this to be a one-pot meal complete with veggies, add frozen peas or fresh snap peas to the pot when after you add the cornstarch slurry and allow to warm through.

BOW TIE PASTA WITH
CHICKEN ALFREDO SAUCE

So many kids love Alfredo sauce. This quick-and-easy recipe cooks the pasta and the chicken together in the pressure cooker, so it's ready in less than 30 minutes. Makes 4 servings.

1 large boneless, skinless chicken breast, diced into bite-size pieces

Salt and freshly ground black pepper

2 tablespoons (28 g) unsalted butter

1 clove of garlic, minced or pressed

2½ cups (570 ml) water

½ teaspoon salt

8 ounces (225 g) bow tie pasta (farfalle)

½ cup (50 g) grated Parmesan cheese, plus more for serving

½ cup (120 ml) heavy cream

2 tablespoons (16 g) cornstarch

2 tablespoons (28 ml) cold water

1 tablespoon (4 g) chopped fresh parsley, optional

1. Lightly season the diced chicken with salt and pepper. Select Sauté to preheat the pressure cooking pot. When the pot is hot, add the butter to melt. Add the chicken and sauté for 3 minutes, stirring occasionally. Add the garlic and sauté for 1 minute more.

2. Add the 2½ cups (570 ml) water and salt to the pressure cooking pot and then stir in the bow tie pasta. Lock the lid in place. Select High Pressure and 4 minutes cook time.

3. When the cook time ends, turn off the pressure cooker. Allow the pressure to release naturally for 3 minutes and then finish with a quick pressure release. (If foam or liquids begin to come from the steam release valve, close it and wait a minute and then try again.) When the float valve drops, carefully remove the lid. Use an instant-read thermometer to check the chicken for doneness (see page 27).

4. Turn off the pressure cooker. Add the Parmesan cheese and stir until melted. Stir in the heavy cream. In a small bowl, combine the cornstarch and 2 tablespoons (28 ml) of cold water and mix well. Select Sauté, pour in the slurry, and simmer, stirring occasionally, until the sauce has

thickened and the pasta is tender, 2 to 3 minutes.

5. Remove the pressure cooking pot from the housing to cool. The sauce will continue to thicken as it cools. (When reheating, you'll need to stir in a little milk to return the sauce to full creaminess.)

6. If your toddler doesn't object to green, stir in the parsley for added color. Scoop into individual bowls and season with additional salt, black pepper, or Parmesan cheese to taste.

TIP

Omit the chicken if you are looking for a meatless meal or stir in frozen chopped veggies and allow to warm through to pump up the nutrition.

CREAMY CHICKEN PESTO PASTA

Known as "green mac and cheese" at our house, this pasta is loaded with fresh vegetables! Using prepared pesto makes this meal come together in a flash! Makes 4 servings.

1 tablespoon (14 g) unsalted butter

1 clove garlic, minced

1 large boneless, skinless chicken breast, cut into bite-size pieces

1 cup (235 ml) reduced-sodium chicken broth

1 cup (235 ml) water

8 ounces (225 g) rotini pasta

½ teaspoon salt, plus more as needed

¼ teaspoon freshly ground black pepper, plus more as needed

2 ounces (55 g) cream cheese, cubed

2 tablespoons (28 ml) milk

1 tablespoon (15 g) prepared pesto

1 cup (124 g) frozen green beans, thawed

½ cup (75 g) grape tomatoes, quartered vertically

1 tablespoon finely chopped fresh (3 g) basil or (4 g) parsley, for serving, optional

Freshly grated mozzarella or Parmesan cheese, for serving

1. Select Sauté to preheat the pressure cooking pot. When the pot is hot, add the butter to melt. Stir in the garlic and cook for 30 seconds. Add the chicken and sauté for 3 minutes, stirring occasionally. Stir in the chicken broth, water, rotini, salt, and pepper. Lock the lid in place. Select High Pressure and 4 minutes cook time.

2. When the cook time ends, turn off the pressure cooker. Let the pressure release naturally for 3 minutes, then finish with a quick pressure release. When the float valve drops, carefully remove the lid. Use an instant-read thermometer to check the chicken for doneness (see page 27).

3. Stir the cream cheese into the hot pasta until melted. Stir in the milk and pesto until blended. Stir in the green beans and cover the pot to steam for 2 minutes or until the green beans are crisp-tender. Mix in the tomatoes and season with salt and pepper to taste.

4. Serve topped with basil and grated mozzarella cheese.

TIP

Although the pesto flavor of this dish is quite mild, for picky toddlers, you can pull out the chicken and pasta right after pressure cooking or after stirring in the milk and cream cheese. You can also substitute your child's favorite vegetable in place of the green beans.

MACARONI AND CHEESE
WITH CHICKEN AND VEGETABLES

Mac and cheese is a classic kid favorite! Feel better about serving it to your toddler by adding chicken and veggies. Makes 4 servings.

1 large boneless, skinless chicken breast, cut into bite-size pieces

Salt and freshly ground black pepper

1 tablespoon (15 ml) vegetable oil

2 cups (475 ml) water

1 teaspoon ground mustard

8 ounces (225 g) elbow macaroni

1 can (12 ounces, or 340 g) evaporated milk

2 cups (225 g) shredded mild cheddar cheese

½ cup (70 g) frozen diced vegetables, such as peas and carrots

Cayenne pepper, Sriracha, or red pepper flakes, for serving, optional

1. Season the diced chicken with salt and pepper. Select Sauté to preheat the pressure cooking pot. When hot, add the vegetable oil and diced chicken. Sauté for 3 minutes, stirring occasionally.

2. Add the water, 1 teaspoon salt, and ground mustard to the pressure cooking pot. Stir in the elbow macaroni. Lock the lid in place. Select High Pressure and 4 minutes cook time.

3. When the cook time ends, turn off the pressure cooker. Allow the pressure to release naturally for 3 minutes and then finish with a quick pressure release. (If foam or liquid begins to come from the pressure release, close it and wait a minute, then try again.) When the float valve drops, carefully remove the lid. Use an instant-read thermometer to check the chicken for doneness (see page 27).

4. Stir in the evaporated milk. Select Sauté and simmer, stirring occasionally, until the pasta is tender, 2 to 3 minutes. (It still might look like too much liquid is in the pot, but it will continue to thicken as it cools.)

5. Turn off the pressure cooker. Add a handful of cheddar cheese and stir until the cheese has melted and the sauce is smooth. Repeat this process one handful at a time until all the cheese is melted and the sauce is smooth. (Adding the cheese all at once will cause the cheese to clump together.)

6. Add the frozen diced vegetables and stir until well combined. Cover with the lid until the vegetables are warmed through, about 3 minutes.

7. Remove the pressure cooking pot from the housing to cool. The sauce will continue to thicken as it cools. (When reheating, you'll need to stir in a little milk to return the mac and cheese to full creaminess.) Season with additional salt, black pepper, cayenne pepper, Sriracha, or red pepper flakes to taste.

TIP

Bacon is a nice addition to the parent portion. Simply dice the bacon and then add it to the pressure cooking pot. Select Sauté and cook, stirring occasionally, until the bacon is crisp. Use a slotted spoon to quickly remove the bacon to a paper towel–lined plate. Then, sauté the diced chicken in the remaining bacon fat, adding up to 1 tablespoon (15 ml) of vegetable oil as needed. Continue with the recipe as directed and sprinkle on the crisp bacon just prior to serving.

SAUCE-SEPARATE LASAGNA

The sauce in this recipe is made separately in case your toddler is picky. Cottage cheese has a milder flavor than ricotta and a higher moisture content, making it perfect for this Sauce-Separate Lasagna recipe. Makes 4 servings.

8 ounces (225 g) country-style sausage

1 can (14.5 ounces, or 410 g) diced tomatoes, well drained

1 can (8 ounces, or 225 g) tomato sauce

1 teaspoon garlic powder

1 teaspoon dried basil

⅛ teaspoon red pepper flakes

¼ teaspoon salt

1 cup (225 g) plus 3 tablespoons (42 g) cottage cheese, divided

1½ cups (173 g) shredded mozzarella cheese, divided

½ cup (40 g) shredded Parmesan cheese

Nonstick cooking spray

6 no-boil lasagna noodles

1 cup (235 ml) water

1. Select Sauté to preheat the pressure cooking pot. When the pot is hot, add the sausage. Cook for about 5 minutes, stirring frequently to break up the meat, until the sausage is no longer pink. Drain any excess fat from the pot. Stir in the tomatoes, tomato sauce, garlic powder, basil, red pepper flakes, and salt. Transfer to the top stackable stainless steel pan and set aside. Wipe out the pressure cooking pot.

2. In a large bowl, mix together 1 cup (225 g) cottage cheese, 1 cup (115 g) of mozzarella cheese, and the Parmesan cheese until blended. Spray the bottom stackable stainless steel pan with nonstick cooking spray. Spread the remaining 3 tablespoons (42 g) of cottage cheese on the bottom of the prepared pan. Break the noodles into pieces to form a single layer on top of the cottage cheese. Spread half of the cheese mixture on top of the cottage cheese. Add a second layer of noodles and the remaining cheese mixture. Top with a third layer of noodles and sprinkle with the remaining ½ cup (60 g) mozzarella cheese. Cover the pan with aluminum foil.

3. Add 1 cup (235 ml) water to the cooking pot. Place the double-stack pan in the pot. Lock the lid in place. Select High Pressure and 20 minutes cook time.

4. When the cook time ends, turn off the pressure cooker. Let the pressure release naturally for 10 minutes and then finish with a quick pressure release. When the float valve drops, carefully remove the lid. Remove the pan from the cooking pot and let rest for 5 minutes prior to serving.

TIP
If you want to prepare the sauce on the stovetop, you can double the recipe and cook lasagna in both the top and the bottom stacked pans. If you don't have a stackable stainless steel cooking pan, you can cook the sauce on the bottom of the pressure cooking pot and prepare the lasagna in a 7-inch (18 cm) cake pan. Place the cake pan on a trivet directly above the sauce and cook as directed.

ROTINI WITH MEATLESS MARINARA SAUCE

Kids will often try sauces if you give them a separate bowl filled with sauce for them to dip their noodles into, so this recipe cooks the sauce in a separate bowl on top of your pasta. Some toddlers are picky about having meat in their pasta sauce; however, if your toddler likes meat sauce, add some browned ground beef. Makes 4 servings.

2½ cups (570 ml) water, plus more as needed

8 ounces (225 g) rotini pasta

Marinara Sauce

1 can (14.5 ounces, or 406 g) crushed tomatoes

1 tablespoon (7 g) grated fresh carrot

½ teaspoon garlic powder

½ teaspoon dried basil

½ teaspoon salt

Freshly ground black pepper

Red pepper flakes, optional

1. Add the water and rotini to the pressure cooking pot. Make sure the water covers the rotini. Place a trivet on top of the rotini.

2. *Prepare the Marinara Sauce:* In a 7-inch (18 cm) cake pan, stir together the tomatoes, grated carrot, garlic powder, basil, and salt. Use a sling to carefully lower the pan onto the trivet. Lock the lid in place. Select High Pressure and 4 minutes cook time.

3. When the cook time ends, turn off the pressure cooker. Use a quick pressure release. If foam or liquid begins to come from the pressure release, close it and wait a minute, then try again. When the float valve drops, carefully remove the lid.

4. Use the sling to remove the pan from the cooking pot. Remove the trivet. Use a slotted spoon to scoop the rotini into bowls. The Marinara Sauce will continue to thicken as it cools. Season with additional salt, black pepper, or red pepper flakes to taste.

TIP

The grated carrot adds sweetness and extra vegetables to the sauce; if you'd like, you can add more to your taste or omit it. If you don't want to grate the carrot, you can also roast or boil it and mash it before adding to the Marinara Sauce.

CHICKEN RISOTTO AND FRESH VEGETABLES

Cooking risotto is so much easier in the pressure cooker than on the stove. Pressure cooker risotto comes out smooth and creamy and lets you skip all the stirring and adding liquids in batches. This smooth and creamy risotto is loaded with chicken and fresh veggies to make a full meal. Makes 4 servings.

1 large boneless, skinless chicken breast, diced

Salt and freshly ground black pepper

¼ teaspoon dried marjoram herbes de Provence, rosemary, or basil

4 to 5 tablespoons (55 to 70 g) unsalted butter, divided, plus more if necessary

10 fresh asparagus spears, trimmed and cut into 2-inch (5 cm) pieces

½ medium zucchini, thinly sliced

½ yellow squash, thinly sliced

1 tablespoon (15 ml) olive oil

½ cup (80 g) diced onion

1½ cups (270 g) Arborio rice

1 tablespoon (9 g) capers, optional

2¼ cups (535 ml) reduced-sodium chicken broth

2 to 4 tablespoons (28 to 60 ml) fresh lemon juice

1 tablespoon (6 g) lemon zest

1 cup (80 g) finely shredded Parmesan cheese, plus more for serving

½ cup (55 g) freshly grated fontina cheese

1 tablespoon (1 g) dried parsley

1. Generously season the chicken with salt, pepper, and herbs. Set aside.

2. Select Sauté to preheat the pressure cooking pot. When the pot is hot, melt 1 tablespoon (14 g) of the butter in the cooking pot. Add the asparagus spears and sauté for 2 minutes. Add the zucchini and squash slices and sauté for 1 minute more. Transfer the vegetables from the pressure cooking pot to a platter and cover.

3. Add 1 tablespoon (14 g) butter and 1 tablespoon (15 ml) olive oil to the cooking pot. Add the chicken and brown for 2 minutes. Remove the browned chicken to a platter.

4. Add 1 tablespoon (14 g) butter to the pressure cooking pot. Add the onion and cook, stirring often, for about 1 minute. Add the rice and sauté for 3 minutes. Add another 1 tablespoon (14 g) butter if needed. Add the capers, if using, and cook for 1 minute more.

5. Add the chicken broth. Add the chicken with any accumulated juices, lemon juice, and lemon zest. Lock the lid in place. Select High Pressure and 5 minutes cook time.

6. When the cook time ends, turn off the pressure cooker. Use a quick pressure release. When the float valve drops, carefully remove the lid. Use an instant-read thermometer to check the chicken for doneness (see page 27).

7. Stir in the Parmesan and fontina cheese, parsley, and 1 tablespoon (14 g) butter. Stir in the sautéed vegetables and heat through. Serve immediately, topped with Parmesan, if desired.

TIP
This meal cooks up thick to make it easier for toddlers to eat. If you'd like a thinner consistency, add more chicken broth before serving.

EASY PORK CHOPS IN GRAVY

This old-fashioned, family-favorite recipe has been passed down from generation to generation. Our family called it "pork chops the long way" before we updated it for the pressure cooker. The pork chops are so tender, you can use a fork to chop them into bite-size toddler pieces. Makes 4 servings.

4 boneless pork loin chops, about 1 inch (2.5 cm) thick

Lemon pepper or your favorite spice blend, for seasoning

1 tablespoon (15 ml) vegetable oil

2¾ cups (650 ml) water, divided

1 can (10.5 ounces, or 295 g) condensed cream of mushroom soup

1 cup (185 g) white rice

2 tablespoons (16 g) all-purpose flour, optional

3 tablespoons (45 ml) cold water, optional

1. Pat the pork chops dry and season liberally with lemon pepper. Select Sauté to preheat the pressure cooking pot. When the pot is hot, add the vegetable oil. When the oil begins to sizzle, add 2 chops and brown for about 2 minutes per side. Transfer to a platter and repeat with the remaining 2 chops.

2. Add 1½ cups (355 ml) water to deglaze the pot, scraping up any browned bits from the bottom. Stir in the cream of mushroom soup. Add the pork chops and any accumulated juices.

3. Place a trivet in the bottom of the pressure cooking pot over the pork chops. In a 7-inch (18 cm) cake pan, stir together the rice and remaining 1¼ cups (295 ml) water. Use a sling to carefully lower the pan onto the rack. Lock the lid in place. Select High Pressure and 4 minutes cook time.

4. When the cook time ends, turn off the pressure cooker. Let the pressure release naturally for 10 minutes, then finish with a quick pressure release. When the float valve drops, carefully remove the lid. Use the sling to remove the pan from the cooking pot. Remove the trivet. Use an instant-read thermometer to check the pork for doneness (see page 27). Transfer the pork chops to a large serving bowl.

5. If you prefer a thicker gravy, select Sauté and whisk the flour into the 3 tablespoons (45 ml) cold water in a small bowl until smooth. Add 1 cup (235 ml) gravy to the flour mixture and stir until well combined. Slowly stir this mixture into the gravy in the cooking pot. Cook, stirring constantly, until thickened to the desired consistency. Pour the gravy over the chops and rice to serve.

TIP

If you prefer a thicker gravy, increase the flour slurry to 4 tablespoons (31 g) flour with 5 tablespoons (75 ml) cold water and then continue with the recipe as directed. Be sure to allow time for the flour to cook over medium heat until bubbly to get the full thickening effect.

CUBED BEEF AND GRAVY
OVER NOODLES

These fall-apart-in-your-mouth pieces of sirloin and flavorful gravy are served over egg noodles. Adding sour cream is optional, but many toddlers love the flavor and even use it as a dip for steamed veggies. Makes 4 servings.

1 to 2 tablespoons (15 to 28 ml) vegetable oil

2 pounds (900 g) beef sirloin tip roast, cubed

¼ cup (40 g) finely diced onion

1 cup (235 ml) reduced-sodium beef broth

1 cube beef bouillon, optional

¼ to ½ cup (31 to 63 g) all-purpose flour

1 cup (235 ml) warm water

Salt and freshly ground black pepper

1 package (16 ounces, or 455 g egg) egg noodles, cooked according to package directions

Worcestershire sauce, for serving, optional

Sour cream, for serving, optional

1. Select Sauté and preheat the pressure cooking pot. When the pot is hot, add 1 tablespoon (15 ml) vegetable oil and brown the meat on one side in small batches, adding more oil if needed; do not crowd the pot. Transfer all the browned meat to a plate and then add the onion to the cooking pot and sauté until tender, about 1 minute.

2. Add the beef broth and beef bouillon, if using, to the cooking pot. Add the browned beef and any juices that may have accumulated. Lock the lid in place. Select High Pressure and 15 minutes cook time.

3. When the cook time ends, turn off the pressure cooker. Use a quick pressure release. When the float valve drops, carefully remove the lid. Use an instant-read thermometer to check the beef for doneness (see page 27).

4. In a small bowl, mix the flour and 1 cup (235 ml) warm water to make a slurry to thicken the broth. Stirring constantly, add the slurry to the cooking pot. Select Sauté and bring to a boil. Boil for a few minutes until the gravy is thickened. Add salt and pepper to taste.

5. Serve the beef and gravy over the prepared egg noodles. Top with a splash of Worcestershire sauce and a dollop of sour cream, if desired.

TIP

If you want, you can substitute 1 tablespoon (5 g) dehydrated onion for the diced onion. Just add it with the beef broth after browning the beef.

CREAMY CHICKEN AND RICE SOUP

This creamy soup is made very thick so it's easier for toddlers to eat and features classic flavors the whole family is sure to love. Makes 4 servings.

1 tablespoon (14 g) unsalted butter

½ cup (80 g) chopped onion

½ cup (65 g) diced carrot

½ cup (60 g) diced celery

1 large boneless, skinless chicken breast, diced

2½ cups (570 ml) reduced-sodium chicken broth

6 ounces (170 g) Uncle Ben's Original White Rice

1 tablespoon (1 g) dried parsley

½ teaspoon salt

½ teaspoon freshly ground black pepper

Dash of red pepper flakes, optional

2 tablespoons (16 g) cornstarch

2 tablespoons (28 ml) cold water

3 ounces (85 g) cream cheese, cubed

¼ cup (60 ml) milk

¼ cup (60 ml) half-and-half

1. Select Sauté to preheat the pressure cooking pot. When the pot is hot, add the butter to melt. Add the onion, carrot, and celery. Sauté for about 5 minutes, stirring occasionally, until the vegetables are tender. Stir in the chicken, chicken broth, rice, parsley, salt, pepper, and red pepper flakes, if using. Lock the lid in place. Select High Pressure and 5 minutes cook time.

2. When the cook time ends, turn off the pressure cooker. Let the pressure release naturally for 5 minutes, then finish with a quick pressure release. When the float valve drops, carefully remove the lid. Use an instant-read thermometer to check the chicken for doneness (see page 27).

3. In a small bowl, whisk the cornstarch and 2 tablespoons (28 ml) cold water until smooth. Select Sauté and add the slurry to the pot, stirring constantly. Stir in the cream cheese until melted. Stir in the milk and half-and-half and heat through—do not bring to a boil.

TIP

If you prefer, you can thin the adult portions of the soup. After you've removed your toddler's meal, add another ¼ cup (60 ml) milk and ¼ cup (60 ml) half-and-half and then add more chicken broth to reach the desired consistency.

MILD CILANTRO CHICKEN AND AVOCADO SOUP

A chunky chicken soup made with mild chili peppers and served over white rice is a great way to introduce toddlers to different ethnic foods. Makes 4 servings.

Sofrito

3 tablespoons (45 ml) olive oil, divided

1 pasilla or poblano chili pepper, stemmed, seeded, and chopped

1 medium onion, diced

10 cloves garlic, minced or pressed

1 bunch fresh cilantro

Soup

1 tablespoon (15 ml) olive oil

4 boneless, skinless chicken thighs, cut into bite-size pieces

4¼ cups (1 L) water, divided

1 tablespoon (12 g) Caldo de Tomate seasoning, or substitute for 1 bouillon cube and 1 tablespoon (16 g) tomato paste

1 cup (185 g) white rice

1½ tablespoons (23 ml) apple cider vinegar

Diced avocado, for serving

1. *Prepare the sofrito:* Select Sauté to preheat the pressure cooking pot. When the pot is hot, add 1 tablespoon (15 ml) of the olive oil and sauté the pepper, onion, and garlic for 3 to 5 minutes, until tender. Turn off the pressure cooker and transfer the mixture to a blender. Add the cilantro and remaining 2 tablespoons (28 ml) olive oil. Blend until the mixture is the consistency of pesto.

2. *Prepare the soup:* Select Sauté to preheat the pressure cooking pot. When the pot is hot, add the olive oil and sauté the chicken for 3 minutes. Add 3 cups (700 ml) of the water and the seasoning to the pressure cooking pot and stir to dissolve. Place a trivet in the pot over the chicken.

3. In a 7-inch (18 cm) round cake pan, add the rice and remaining 1¼ cups (295 ml) water. Using a sling, carefully lower the pan onto the trivet. Lock the lid in place. Select High Pressure and 4 minutes cook time.

4. When the cook time ends, turn off the pressure cooker. Allow the pressure to release naturally for 10 minutes and then finish with a quick pressure release. When the float valve drops, carefully remove the lid.

5. Use the sling to remove the pan from the pot. Remove the trivet. Add a quarter of the sofrito mixture and the apple cider vinegar to the liquid in the pressure cooking pot. Select Sauté and simmer for 10 minutes.

6. To serve, add a scoop of rice to soup bowls and ladle the soup over the top. Garnish with the avocado.

TIP

The extra sofrito can be stored for up to 1 month. Use it to make another batch of soup—it freezes well—or to make other Mexican-inspired dishes. We like to stir it into fresh rice and serve as a side for tacos.

HEARTY POTATO CHEESE SOUP

This soup is one of the most popular recipes on Pressure Cooking Today—everyone loves the chunky potatoes and the creamy soup! We've thickened the broth and cut the potatoes bite-size so it's a toddler-friendly meal that you'll look forward to eating, too. Makes 4 servings.

1 tablespoon (14 g) plus ⅓ cup (75 g) unsalted butter, divided

¼ cup (40 g) chopped onion

1 can (14.5 ounces, or 410 g) chicken broth

½ teaspoon salt

¼ teaspoon black pepper

Dash of red pepper flakes

1 tablespoon (1 g) dried parsley

3 cups (330 g) peeled and cubed potatoes

2 ounces (55 g) cream cheese, cubed

½ cup (58 g) shredded cheddar cheese

1 cup (235 ml) half-and-half

½ cup (82 g) frozen corn

4 slices crisp-cooked bacon, crumbled

⅓ cup (42 g) all-purpose flour

½ cup (120 ml) milk, plus more as needed

1. Select Sauté to preheat the pressure cooking pot. When the pot is hot, add 1 tablespoon (14 g) butter to melt. Add the onion and cook, stirring occasionally, until tender, about 2 minutes. Add the chicken broth, salt, pepper, red pepper flakes, and parsley and stir to combine.

2. Put the steamer basket in the pressure cooking pot over the broth. Add the cubed potatoes. Lock the lid in place. Select High Pressure and 4 minutes cook time.

3. When the cook time ends, turn off the pressure cooker. Allow the pressure to release naturally for 5 minutes, then finish with a quick pressure release. When the float valve drops, carefully remove the potatoes and steamer basket from the pressure cooking pot.

4. Add the cream cheese and shredded cheddar cheese to the liquid in the pot. Stir until the cheese is melted. Add the half-and-half, corn, crumbled bacon and cooked potatoes, and heat through but do not bring to a boil.

5. In a small saucepan on the stovetop over medium heat, melt the remaining ⅓ cup (75 g) butter. Whisk in the flour. Cook for 2 to 3 minutes, stirring constantly, until smooth and bubbly. Gradually add the milk, stirring constantly, and cook for about 2 minutes until the sauce is thick and smooth. Add this to the pressure cooking pot and stir until the soup is thick and creamy. Add more milk or broth, if needed, to achieve your desired consistency.

TIP

The butter-flour-milk mixture, known as a roux, thickens this soup quite a bit. If you prefer, you can omit it entirely or keep it separate and stir some into your toddler's soup until their portion reaches the desired thickness.

CHAPTER 4

DESSERTS

We don't always serve desserts, but when we want to celebrate a special occasion or milestone, these desserts are easy, fun, and toddler-friendly!

APPLE-BERRY-CHERRY CRISP

Fruit fillings are quick and easy to make in the pressure cooker. By cooking the fruit in the pressure cooker before crisping up the topping in the oven, you cut the cook time by about half. Makes 4 servings.

Nonstick baking spray with flour

4 baking apples, such as Braeburn or Golden Delicious, peeled, cored, and sliced into ¼-inch (6 mm) slices

3 to 4 cups (700 to 946 ml) boiling water

2 cups (310 g) frozen blueberries

1 cup (156 g) frozen cherries

¼ cup (50 g) granulated sugar

1 tablespoon (15 ml) lemon juice

3 tablespoons (24 g) cornstarch

3 tablespoons (45 ml) water

Topping

¼ cup (31 g) all-purpose flour

¼ teaspoon salt

¼ cup (55 g) brown sugar

4 tablespoons (55 g) unsalted butter, cut into small pieces

1 cup (80 g) instant rolled oats

Vanilla ice cream, optional, for serving

1. Preheat the oven to 375°F (190°C, or gas mark 5). Coat an 8 x 8-inch (20 x 20 cm) pan with nonstick baking spray with flour.

2. Place the apple slices in a large bowl or pot. Pour the boiling water directly over the top of the apples. Cover and let sit for 10 minutes. Transfer the apples to a colander and drain well, tossing occasionally until completely dry, about 10 minutes.

3. While the apples are soaking, add the blueberries, cherries, granulated sugar, and lemon juice to the pressure cooking pot and stir to combine. Lock the lid in place and select High Pressure and 2 minutes cook time. When the cook time ends, turn off the pressure cooker. Allow the pressure to release naturally for 10 minutes, then finish with a quick pressure release.

4. In a small bowl, whisk together the cornstarch and 3 tablespoons (45 ml) water. Add the slurry and apples to the pressure cooking pot. Bring to a boil using the Sauté function, stirring constantly. Sauté for 2 minutes.

5. *Prepare the topping:* Meanwhile, in a large bowl, combine the flour, salt, and brown sugar. Using a pastry blender, cut in the butter until large clumps form. Mix in the oats. Set aside.

6. Pour the fruit mixture into the prepared baking dish. Sprinkle the topping mixture evenly on the filling. Place the baking dish on a rimmed baking sheet and bake until the topping is golden brown, about 4 minutes. Let rest for a few minutes before serving.

7. Serve warm, topped with a scoop of vanilla ice cream, if desired.

TIP
To reheat, simply place in a covered bowl and microwave at 50 percent power in 30-second intervals until it reaches your desired temperature.

FRESH BERRIES AND VANILLA CREAM

Having fresh fruit for dessert is a great habit to start. Drizzling a small scoop of the Vanilla Cream over the fruit will have your toddler asking for berries for dessert often! Makes 4 servings.

¾ cup (175 ml) heavy cream

¼ cup (60 ml) milk

2 egg yolks

⅓ cup (67 g) sugar

1 teaspoon vanilla bean paste or extract

4 cups in-season fresh berries ([680 g]sliced strawberries, [500 g] raspberries, [580 g] blueberries, [580 g] blackberries)

1. Select Sauté on your pressure cooker and adjust to low. In the pressure cooking pot, whisk the heavy cream and milk. Cook until the mixture just starts to boil. Remove from the heat.

2. In a medium-size bowl, whisk the egg yolks and sugar until the mixture is pale and thick. Whisk in half the hot milk mixture. Add the egg mixture to the pressure cooking pot, stirring constantly, until the sauce comes to a boil. Turn off the pressure cooker and simmer for about 2 minutes more, stirring constantly. Remove the cooking pot from the housing and stir in the vanilla.

3. Transfer the vanilla cream to a serving bowl or gravy boat and allow to cool. To serve, place berries in small serving dishes and drizzle the Vanilla Cream over the top.

TIP

If your pressure cooker does not adjust to a low heat Sauté setting, you will get best results cooking the Vanilla Cream on your stovetop.

ALEX'S BROWNIE POPS

Apologies to fans of edge pieces—brownies made in the pressure cooker are all middle-piece fudgy chocolate. These rich, moist brownies are perfect for a fun, bite-size treat! Makes 18 to 20 brownie pops.

Nonstick baking spray with flour

1 box (about 20 ounces, or 560 g) family-size fudgy brownie mix (We use Ghirardelli Triple Chocolate.)

1 cup (235 ml) water

18 to 20 lollipop sticks

12 to 16 ounces (340 to 455 g) milk, semisweet, or dark chocolate (We use melting wafers.)

Sprinkles, jimmies, or colorful candy melts, for decoration

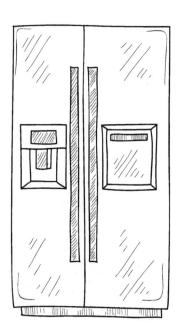

1. Coat a 7-inch (18 cm) springform pan with nonstick baking spray with flour. Set aside.

2. Prepare the brownie mix as directed on the packaging using the recommended oil, water, and eggs for fudgy brownies. (If you're at altitude, be sure to follow the high-altitude directions.) Pour the batter into the prepared pan.

3. Pour 1 cup (235 ml) water into the pressure cooking pot and place a trivet in the bottom. Carefully center the filled pan on a sling and lower the uncovered pan onto the trivet. Lock the lid in place and turn the pressure release switch to the Sealed position. Select High Pressure and 43 minutes cook time.

4. When the cook time ends, turn off the pressure cooker. Let the pressure release naturally for 15 minutes, then finish with a quick pressure release. When the float valve drops, carefully remove the lid. Test the brownies for doneness, either when a toothpick comes out clean or when the brownies spring back when touched gently. Use the sling to transfer the pan to a wire rack and use a paper towel to soak up any water that may have accumulated on top of the brownies or around the sides of the springform pan.

5. Cool for 5 minutes, then slide a thin spatula or knife around the edge of the springform pan to loosen the brownies and open the springform pan. Allow to cool for at least 1 hour.

6. Remove the baked brownies to a large bowl and use a large spoon or your hands to crumble the brownies. Use a #40 cookie scoop (about 1½ tablespoons [23 g]) to scoop the crumbled brownies into balls. Roll with your hands to smooth out the balls and place on a lined baking sheet. Insert a lollipop stick into each brownie ball. Freeze for at least 2 hours or overnight.

7. When ready to decorate, in a microwave-safe dish, heat the chocolate on 50 percent power for 1 minute and then stir. Continue melting and stirring in 30-second intervals until the chocolate is fully melted and smooth.

8. Dip a brownie pop into the melted chocolate. If necessary, use a spoon to completely coat the pop with chocolate and let the excess chocolate drip back into the bowl. Place on the prepared baking sheet. Scatter sprinkles on the chocolate while it is still wet. Repeat with the remaining pops. If the chocolate starts to thicken as it cools, return to the microwave for 15 seconds at 50 percent power. Refrigerate the dipped brownie pops until ready to serve.

TIP

This treat is fun to decorate with your toddler! To reduce mess, put your toddler in charge of sprinkles and place the dipped brownie pops on a lined baking sheet. If your toddler insists on dipping, be aware that you may need more melted chocolate because toddlers tend to dip the chocolate liberally.

Acknowledgments

First, I want to thank all my Pressure Cooking Today readers and members of the various Facebook communities who share their enthusiasm for pressure cooking with me. They keep me energized and striving to create new and innovative recipes and to find new ways to use the electric pressure cooker.

Thank you to my publisher for seeing the need for making toddler food quickly and easily in an electric pressure cooker.

Thanks to my husband, who is my indispensable slicer and dicer in the kitchen. He makes recipe creation so much easier, and he makes it more fun to cook.

Finally, thanks to my amazing, talented daughter who put her heart and soul into this cookbook.

—*Barbara*

This book wouldn't be possible without my family, and I am deeply grateful for them.

First and foremost, to my mother, for your unfailing belief that someone as distracted as me could ever be a good cook. Thank you for inviting me to help in your kitchen and with your websites. I am so grateful for the opportunities you've provided me and am thrilled to join you on this pressure cooking journey.

To my father, for being happy to help however needed, from lending a hand in the kitchen to watching my boys so I could write.

To my boys, for happily suggesting recipe ideas, taste-testing recipes, and providing candid feedback. Thank you for eating toddler meals for breakfast, lunch, and dinner and for snacks and dessert. I love watching you grow and can't wait to see what you do next.

And finally, to my husband, whose contributions to this cookbook are innumerable and whose steady support made it possible. You are truly my partner on this journey, and I just adore you.

—*Jennifer*

About the Authors

Barbara Schieving Barbara Schieving is a veteran mom of four grown children. She is widely admired cook, writer, and photographer whose two blogs, *Pressure Cooking Today* and *Barbara Bakes*, delight over half a million readers each month with her fabulous, family-friendly recipes and conversational style. Her most recent cookbook, *Instantly Sweet* (2018), written with Marci Buttars, introduces readers to the sweet side of electric pressure cooking, with 75 delicious desserts and sweet treats. Her other cookbooks include *The Electric Pressure Cooker Cookbook* (2017), which features 200 delicious recipes made pressure-cooker fast with fresh and familiar ingredients, and *Simply Sweet Dream Puffs* (2015), which features a wide variety of easy-to-make cream puffs, eclairs, and profiteroles. She lives in the Salt Lake City, Utah, area.

Jennifer Schieving McDaniel is a busy mother of three. She fell in love with pressure cooking when she and her husband lived with her parents while building a new home and is now a huge pressure cooker enthusiast. She uses her pressure cooker every day, often several times a day, to prepare nutritious family meals and can't wait to make these recipes for the little one who recently joined their family. Jennifer and her husband love sharing their pressure cooking expertise and often teach friends, family, and groups how easy it is to cook great meals in the pressure cooker. Jennifer is the managing editor for *Pressure Cooking Today* and is an integral part of the *Pressure Cooking Today* team. She creates recipes, writes how-to posts, answers readers' questions, and so much more. She lives near Barbara in the Salt Lake City, Utah, area.

INDEX

CPSIA information can be obtained
at www.ICGtesting.com
Printed in the USA
LVHW022204051218
599381LV00002B/2